Member
HEAL
Thyself

Member
HEAL
Thyself

R. Shelton, NLMT, BCTMB

Member Heal Thyself

For Those Beginning to

Take an Active Part in Healing Their

Heart, Mind, and Soul

And Live Closer to Wholeness

Every Day

Acknowledgements

I'd like to thank God, my Father in Heaven, for leading me down this path and prompting me to write this book. I would not be where I am today without him. He has taught me through the process of writing this book that my life is a miracle. I hope this book will make him proud.

Next, I thank my loving, supportive husband. He's been a great help to me and a living example of love, light, and forgiveness. My moral support and always there for me, he is a gift in my life every day. I love you, my darling!

To my amazing child who inspires and challenges me: you are the sunshine in my day; you are, have always been, and will always be a great blessing in my life. Always remember how precious you are! Helping you achieve your dreams has taught me courage to keep moving forward with mine too. You amaze me.

I'd like to thank my family and friends; and those who have graduated from this life. Thank you for helping shape who I am today. I value your friendship, life lessons, wisdom and experiences.

I'd especially like to thank those who have given permission to share parts of their stories here. Coming from difficult circumstances does not mean there is no hope to heal. In fact, usually this is a sign that change is possible. This book shows how to overcome challenges with help. I will cover some of the things I and my clients have successfully used in this book. I have changed names, personal details, and locations for privacy of individuals.

Many thanks to my clients for all you have taught me. You have shown great trust in me in supporting this work. You have blessed my life, and I have seen you in turn reach out and help those around you. The effects have rippled out to those who observe you, and the changes you have made in your lives each day. Each one of you has touched my life, and I treasure the gifts and insights I received from and through you.

To those who helped me through the publishing process thank you. The many hours of cover work, mentoring on the publishing process and writing will bless the lives of many. Thank you for holding my hand! I would have been so lost.

Last but not least, I thank *you*. It takes courage to move forward in your life, to embrace the joy that God has for you. I hope you find some gem of knowledge in these pages that will bless your life or the life of someone you know. Find hope and strength to keep moving forward. Trust God's plan for your life whether or not you are ready to believe that he has one for you. It is my sure witness to you he does. You can only begin to see as you clear out some of the clutter.

We know the importance of spring cleaning our homes. Spring cleaning our emotions is as important for our wellness. Reach that place for yourself. Do not give up when you feel despair on your journey. It is a sign you are ready or you need someone to help you. Work is always easier with help. Don't be afraid to start now. Your time is now. I don't (can't!) believe in coincidences. I have seen too often all things work out to our benefit. Timing is no coincidence. You will get there; keep moving forward one step at a time.

Special Note

The three stories shared in the first three chapters of this book are separate experiences. Each of these chapters is written about a different trauma or set of traumas in need of massage and other healing modality interventions. These stories are being shared with you in the hopes that it will help you in your own healing journey. The names, locations, and other personal details have been altered to protect the individual's privacy and the privacy of their families.

Contents

Acknowledgements

Special Note

Contents

Chapter 1
Cancer

I REMEMBER HOW LIFE WAS in the Jones family before the cancer. I remember a time before my sister was born. My mom and dad were thinner, younger, and more energetic, and life seemed to be perfect. People would come over for dinner, or to visit, and my family would do things for fun on a regular basis. I would play and feel so carefree and I knew I was safe and loved. The world was a happy place to be.

Dad went to school to be an engineer while in the military. I remember when he cut his hair so short. It was very disturbing to me, and I didn't recognize him at all. I felt very uncomfortable until I got used to it. Dad had to train and practice with his gun. Sometimes, very rarely, I got to go to the shooting range with him. It was pretty special to do something together. He would go on hunting and fishing trips with my uncles and his friends sometimes. He got interested in greenhouses for a side business. Eventually, this led him to an interest in growing plants. We had a little patch of grass in our yard where Dad would play with us. At times he brought home inner tubes and rolled us around in the yard. Sometimes he even gave us horsey back rides.

My mom was great too. She made the most delicious meals I ever tasted. The kitchen often smelled of chocolate chip cookies, blueberry pancakes, or muffins. In the summer she always made homemade popsicles for us to eat. She smiled and laughed a lot back then and her eyes would sparkle when she did. Her hair was always well put together and shined like she'd stepped out of a hair commercial. Mom had a glow and a quiet way that would light up whatever room she was in. She captivated people.

My mom would get so excited about the holidays. They were something wonderful, and we looked forward to them. We knew there would be goodies and gifts, visitors, barbecues, and games. Even when times were far humbler, my mom had a way of making everything feel magical. She was the best story teller. We piled around her and listened completely encompassed in the warmth of her love. I'm sure I had my share of disappointments and tantrums growing up, but I felt happy and loved. Every need was being met in my life.

I loved being an only child but I reached a point where I realized my life would be much more fun with a sibling. After careful consideration, as much as a two-year-old can muster, I decided that I needed a brother. I approached my parents about my desire and a while later, along came two brothers. I felt alarmed at first getting two for the price of one. But I soon forgot my shock realizing these new squishy playmates would be more fun than I had hoped.

After a year passed, the boys were more interested in each other than in me. This was when I decided I needed a sister to even things out. I needed someone to share things and visit with - to do girly things with. After careful consideration, I approached my parents with my request. It worked like the candy machine at the grocery store, or so I thought. Dad put some money in the vending machine and turned the handle, and I got a prize!

Along came the baby sister I ordered. I cherished her as well, and my life was now complete.

Once my sister was born, I told my parents everything was perfect. I didn't need any more brothers or sisters. They could stop there with the babies: all I needed was two brothers and one sister. I was so content with everything in my life!

It seemed only a few short months passed, and my mom was expecting another baby but I hadn't requested another one. What were my parents doing? My parents laughed delighted at my naivety. Soon another set of twins arrived and I didn't know what to do!

Near the time of my sister's birth, my life shattered around me. Due to things that happened, I felt I had no hope of repair or the will to continue living. Later in adulthood, I learned that I became emotionally stunted at that age due to trauma. I was unable to progress beyond that age until I was able to find the help I needed.

My parents discovered my sister's life was at stake. I learned what a terminal illness meant for her. It would take decades to realize that it would affect our whole family. My relationship with my parents changed. I felt abandoned and forgotten. I did everything I could think of to please them to try and get that relationship back. As an adult I learned that one of the causes of allergies is emotions. One of my parents had developed an emotional allergy to me. It was a bad enough allergy that it also created a physical reaction. At the time, none of us knew what was going on. Today there are allergy elimination treatments available that can reverse these reactions. It's not discussed a lot as many people have not heard of them. They're very effective, but they were not available then.

After my sister became ill, I started feeling displaced. I felt my parents no longer wanted me. I felt betrayed and unloved. *I* had asked for this sister and was getting no credit for the child that my mother had told me was mine. I couldn't understand how this other child could be far more precious to my parents. I couldn't figure out where I had gone wrong. This replacement did not seem to translate to my brothers. I decided this was the biggest mistake I had ever made. I wanted an immediate refund! At my very young age I thought everything and everyone revolved around me, my wants and needs.

More traumas, unrelated to my sister, occurred in my life, and I lost all confidence in my parents. I realized I could not trust them to keep their word. I no longer believed what they had taught me, and I felt more alone than ever. I had no one to rely on any longer. I paced this prison, this cage, until I could finally escape. I had repeated proof that no one had my back. I realized no one would ever hold me like I was the most precious person to them. There would be no one to make me feel safe, loved, and wanted ever again. It was now me against the world. I once believed the world was a safe and happy place. I learned it was full of darkness, misery, and fear. I was surrounded by people but completely alone.

My family tells a beautiful, heart-wrenching story about my sister's cancer. They rushed her to the doctor and then drove her over to the Michigan Medical Center. The surgeons at the center got her right into surgery. They did an emergency biopsy to try and figure out what they were dealing with. We were all waiting in the recovery room for her to wake up from the anesthesia. When she did, she looked over at me and called out my name as she reached for me. Everyone gushed about how wonderful it was that she called for her big sister.

I could tell you that story word for word because I've heard it repeated many times. Every time it grated against my ears and pierced my heart with guilt and anger. I wanted to scream at them to stop telling the story. No one knew what it was doing to me. They didn't know what had been going on in my head and my heart as they forced me to sit next to my sister's bed. If they had known my thoughts, they would have locked me up and never have told the story again. It would have been the story of a miracle child who made people believe in God again. Then there would be the untold story of her older sister who wanted her to die.

I have never told anyone my version of the story. When someone asked me to write it down after I had gone through a lot of healing, my first response was to say no. The anonymity of my story gave me the courage to tell it so it might help someone else. Massage treatments have been an important part of my healing process. I found out that I could renew and restore myself to happiness. This is my version of the story.

My parents took my sister to the family doctor. He told them to take this sick child straight to the medical center several hours away. The doctor told them not to stop for gas or the police under any circumstances. He would call ahead for them to let the hospital and the police know they were coming. My mom and dad dropped the rest of us off at Grandma's house. We stayed there until they said it was okay for us to come. It might have been the next day. My sister would be out of surgery by the time we got there.

Driving to the medical center seemed to take forever. In the days of no kids allowed in hospitals, I remember my grandmother not taking no for an answer from anyone. She brought us straight into the room where my sister lay unconscious. No one dared challenge Grandma once she put her foot down. My parents were waiting for my sister to wake up from the anesthesia. Mom was unable to hide the tears brimming in her eyes as we came up to the doorway. They waited to hear if there would be anything the doctors could do to help. No one would be able to tell how she was doing until she woke up. The doctors were working on the samples they had collected. They hoped they might shed some light on the situation.

Visitors, especially children, were never allowed in the hospital back then. Too noisy and too many germs weren't good for healing, they said. Everyone exchanged tense hugs. The adults shushed our childish questions about if our sister was all right. She was resting and we weren't to wake her. We obeyed but remained observant for clues about what was going on. We strained to hear what the adults were discussing in whispered tones. We didn't understand what was going on but we knew it was a very big deal. She had something bad and she could die.

There was only room for one hard plastic chair crammed between the hospital bed and the door in the tiny room. We tried to fit three adults and three squirmy kids in that small cupboard of a room. We did our best not to stick out into the hallway as the nurses rushed about. The situation was uncomfortable in every way. There was no way I was going to take that only chair next to the bed my sister was lying in. She looked like she might never wake up. With all those tubes and hoses coming out of her she looked like an alien to me. It terrified me! I had never seen anyone like that before. Seeing and feeling the alarm of the adults and the way the nurses reacted only added to my fear.

I didn't want to be anywhere close to that hospital bed. I wished I wasn't even in that hospital at all! My sister, through no fault of her own, seemed to be the main reason my world was falling apart. I wanted nothing to do with this! The last place I wanted to be was in the chair next to the bed.

I thought about all the others in the room and tried to figure out how to get someone to sit in the chair. That would make it seem farther away from me and then I wouldn't have to be the one to sit in it. I respected my grandmother too much not to let her have the chair. She was old and deserved to sit in it and I could feel noble.

Then I thought of my parents. Their place should be next to their dying child. I knew my father would let Mom have the chair. He was a gentleman and always opened the door for her and got her chair at the table. Mom should be closer to her beautiful baby. Finally, I thought of my brothers. They were younger and small enough they could share the seat. They were so sweet too. I would be glad to let them have the chair. They weren't as strong as I was and would get tired faster. That would leave one free arm for my father to put around mother and one arm for me while we waited.

The lone, obnoxious hospital chair seemed to taunt me until I almost panicked. I remember wishing there had been an extra chair on the far side of the room. I could sneak behind the long thick curtains by the window on the opposite wall. If I could slip behind them, I knew I would disappear. I tried to hide my sore feet and tired legs by shifting my weight a little. The adults began to notice and suggested I sit in the chair. I declined as the time dragged on until they forced me into it.

I sat on the edge of the chair as far from the bed as I could without being too obvious how horrified I was to be there. I felt anger and resentment towards everyone. The adults were whispering about possible outcomes. I began to feel hopeful that she would not wake up. I began to pray in secret, pleading with God, while perched on that awful chair. I felt like a vulture waiting for the inevitable chance to gorge itself on the carcass of prey. From what I hoped was an innocent place in my heart, I hoped this thing would prove to me that he wanted me to be happy again.

I didn't want this perfect, beautiful baby to die. I didn't want her to feel any pain or loss. But I could only imagine my parents would only love me if I was the only girl in the family again. I believed there was no other way. I wanted to feel safe, happy, and loved and for no one to ever know that any of them had hurt me so much. Being loved can be a strong motivator.

The nurses told us we could actually see the tumor grow if we watched it. The cancer was doubling in size every few hours. Everyone else was waiting for the grand awakening. To hold off my boredom as the hours dragged on, I focused on the cancer to see it grow. I watched and I waited for everyone's disappointment when my sister didn't wake up.

A short time before, I sat up late with my father on a camping trip. We talked about the constellations as he pointed them out to me. We listened to the fire dying down. The earthworms were coming up to munch on the dead plants from last fall. I remember my dad showed me how to pay attention to the green grass and that I would see it move and change. I saw the grass growing longer and it had shocked me! He told me about how it grows faster at night. It was an amazing thing to learn.

As I sat in the hospital room watching my sister against a fixed point on the wall, I saw the cancer grow. It seemed to be moving faster than the grass had that night by the camp fire. This was some weird freakish thing inside of my sister! I knew she would be better off if she died, and it would be a merciful act. I remembered the screams of actors in a recent horror film advertised on television. A creature tore itself out of a woman impregnated by an alien creature when it had come to full term. We didn't see that movie, but I remembered the commercial as I sat there.

I hated it that I hated her so much. She was beautiful and sweet and kind and that made it so much harder to hate her. I didn't know then I was in survival mode. The added confusion of the guilt I felt was more than I could bear. Now I prayed to God to let my sister die out of mercy. I loved her so much it hurt, and I didn't want her to suffer. My thoughts then turned to myself. I had to survive, and it didn't seem like it was going to happen. If I loved my sister and she lived I knew I would lose my parents' love and disappear forever.

Time stretched on after seeing the cancer grow, and I began to zone out. Without warning - almost in slow motion - my sister started to turn her head away from the window. Her delicate curls were the perfect color. It was a vision seeing them catching the warm sunlight like heaven's promise. She turned her head away from the light toward the cold fluorescent side of the room. Her eyes, trusting and relaxed, searched for familiar faces. We were all crammed between her and the door.

Page 12

I was the closest, so I was the first person that she saw. She didn't even seem to notice anyone else in the room. She gasped my name, voice weak and cracking from the anesthesia. She reached her delicate little arms towards me. Pure joy filled her face to see her big sister there. It took me by surprise and before I could react, everyone started choking up. They began crying and commenting at how much she loved her big sister. The huge wave of guilt that came crashing down caused me to cower inside and wish I could die.

How wonderful, yes, how lovely, yes, everyone proclaimed. All I could think about was my train of thought the last few hours. Yes, the "dutiful" sister. Hot tears came to my eyes; great tears of unforgivable guilt. My shame lodged deep into my soul. My sister had survived the biopsy and that meant she might survive the cancer too. I swore a promise to myself. I would have to be the best big sister. No one would try harder than I would. If I did a good enough job, I would convince myself I was not a bad person. Someday I would even believe it myself.

I swore to myself that no one would ever know my thoughts. I stood to take her hand at her bedside and said, "Yes, I'm here!" I smiled at her through my bitter tears as I choked back spiteful contempt. Everyone rushed the bed to hug the little toddler, pushing me out of the way. I was angry, in shock, and full of resentment and that horrified me. To me, this frail young toddler was the pride and joy of my parents. The hospital had tied her down with medical tubes and tape to the hospital bed, like a sacrifice on an altar. I soon discovered my family would spend the rest of our lives worshipping her. She was now my secret enemy.

I thought for most of my life that keeping my hurt, angry feelings and thoughts a secret would be a good thing. My health declined over decades from causes medical science could not explain. Their prescribed medications only made things worse. I discovered massage therapy late in adulthood. I learned through the treatments that keeping dark secrets makes things worse. You have to deal with them either way. They have a way of finding their way out no matter what you do so you might as well address them and get it over with. Trapped emotions can show up as sadness or depression, and tiredness. They can even appear as various forms of dis-ease, even nervous breakdowns. Unless you get the proper help and release these feelings, they will get worse. They can change with proper treatments. I found massage to be very effective to help my body do this.

I felt like it would take a lifetime of servitude to reverse the effects of my anger. I did my best to do what my parents asked of me. I tried to honor their individual requests to help support the other parent. They were both often absent from the home as they focused every resource they had to save my sister's life. A total of five unplanned pregnancies came over the next seven years. This included another set of twins. The new twins both died not more than a year or two after my sister's terminal diagnosis. It was a time of great distress and devastation for my whole family. Some of us seemed to be more affected than others, but we all attempted to hide our problems.

My parents asked me to take over the mothering role, so I changed diapers. I stood in as the main comforter every time we were all farmed out to anyone willing to take on nine kids. We'd stay with host families for a few days up to a week at a time. Our parents had to travel out of town to get to the cancer center for my sister's treatments for the next decade. They had never seen this type of cancer before and they weren't taking any chances. Few people are willing to take on that many extra kids for a whole week or two on top of their own. It was a time of ongoing uncertainty for the whole family. I did my best to try to soothe scared and homesick siblings. They wanted their mother and didn't understand where she was or why she hadn't returned to them at the end of each day. They focused their frustration on me since I was there.

Our hosts were unable to soothe the youngest children, though they made very valiant efforts to do so. We were in unfamiliar territory. Strange habits surrounded us and lots of cooking we weren't accustomed to. We felt afraid all the time, and so everything new scared us even more. We didn't know the host children at times and had to share beds and sleep on the floor. Some of the homes were friendlier. Others reeked with hostility, threats, and abuse. Some of the host children delighted in being cruel to us. It was my job to keep all my siblings safe. I felt inadequate and unprepared. They thrust me into an unwanted role without warning or training.

I laid awake and afraid late into the night at some of those houses. Every strange noise would jerk me awake, prepared for a battle. It seemed impossible to get back to sleep. I learned scary things happen in the dark. Still a child myself, I didn't know what I could do against enemies bigger and stronger than I was. I took my job to protect my siblings with great seriousness. I had learned by experience, adults rarely offered any real protection for children. It was up to me. Deprived of sleep many nights, I'd get up and help my siblings get ready for the day. I'd often struggle to stay awake at school and had to keep up with my classmates and maintain good grades.

Grandma's house was by far the best place for us to stay. It was the most familiar to us. We spent a lot of time at her house even when Mom and Dad were home. Grandma would help my mom have a break from us kids, rub my mom's feet, and talk or listen to her. She'd give her vitamins to help with her stress and feed us all dinner. She'd give us all vitamins to help us grow up to be strong. We were often sent outside which allowed the adults to talk about grown up things. It was in these fleeting moments I could let my adult responsibilities go and run free until it was time to go home. I loved how the wind felt when I ran. The wind seemed to caress my face and hair, and I felt strong and alive. I felt loved like before the cancer. If I ran fast enough, I could outrun my troubles and they would never catch me again.

I could feel the dark heaviness of my responsibilities settling over me as we drove back home. It seemed there was no hope of escape. Even when my parents *were* home, they didn't seem to be mentally there much of the time. They were too overwhelmed. As their hearts failed them with each added tragedy, my parents turned away from each other. They turned away from us towards their own private escapes and we were even more alone. The last fibers holding the family together strained until they threatened to snap.

People felt sorry for our family and said, "The poor Jones family, the poor Joneses; what can we do for them?" My parents always said there was nothing anyone could do other than offer moral support. That's the worst thing you can tell people. Then they can't and won't do anything for you. It's not because they don't want to help either. People don't know what to do and think you're telling them you don't want their help at all. That's kind of a slap in the face to someone who offers you a kind gift of service and love. They didn't know what to do for us because they had never been through what we were experiencing. My parents also didn't realize how much they needed help - or what kind. I know I needed help but their words silenced my voice. Sometimes helping with things you "don't need help with" is even help. Clean the toilet, wash some dishes, or sweep a floor. It shows you care and want to support them.

My parents swore the family to secrecy about how difficult things were for us. From that point on, it was as if it was our fault if people could see our need - and it was a bad thing. Self-sufficiency is good, but admitting your limitations is okay. It's also okay to let people lend a helping hand. They shouldn't do for you what you can do yourself, but it's never a bad thing to let people know you love them. It does not diminish you as long as you are honest about your effort. Anyone who tries to tell you otherwise is operating from a place of fear, not from love.

We children were to put on a smile and tell everyone that everything was fine. It wouldn't do for people to feel bad for us since there was nothing they could do. Today, you see people raising funds to help people and moral support going viral on social media. People today cannot imagine a time like the one I endured, but it was my experience growing up. I wasn't angry like they thought, I was tired. Tired and so frustrated. I had no one to talk to, but I needed someone. I needed a village of supporters to help me know everything was going to be all right.

We have come a long way in offering help today. There are people all around us who are lonely and dealing with difficult challenges. They feel alone and need help and friendship. Reach out to them. You may save someone's life. My situation is not unique. I wasn't allowed to talk to anyone in my extended family and definitely not to anyone outside the family. Get to know people well enough, and go with your feeling that they might need your help.

Church camps and school reinforced to me that I could not count on adults to take care of me.

I had to maintain the illusion of independence and self-sufficiency. I had to be good enough at everything so I wouldn't raise suspicion. But I couldn't be too good at anything, either. My parents' extra burdens would be too great if they had to do anything for me. I couldn't be myself at a time in my life when I should have been figuring out who I was. I had to figure out how to lie to people and make them believe everything was fine. I felt terrified most of the time. If anyone found out, I or my family might break into a million pieces. It was all I could do to keep people the right distance away to protect my glass castle at all times. There was no end in sight to the deception about how we were doing.

I became dead to my emotions aside from breakdowns twice a year. I could not afford to feel. I once had dreams to run in the Olympics, and I started bringing home fliers from school. Mother glanced at them without looking. She always told me I could not take part. No matter how lame her excuses were or how much I was able to overcome them, she never let me do anything I loved. When I exhausted her excuses, she began attacking me on an emotional level until I fled. She made me feel "less than." Gone were the days of goodness between us. It was devastating to me. Every time I asked her to let me take part in something, she treated me even worse.

Over the next few years I tried my best to help everyone and not complain. I kept asking to be part of sports teams and other available groups with no success. My brothers were almost always allowed to do anything they wanted. It didn't matter if there were ongoing expenses. Our parents would sign the boys up without question. They *told* me they believed in equal opportunities for girls and boys since I could remember. But what they said and what they did were complete opposites. This fueled my resentment.

I did all kinds of footwork for fundraisers to pay for my expenses. I had people lined up who volunteered to car-pool me if my own parents weren't able to take me. They would help me provide for all my needs so my parents wouldn't have to lift a single finger. I told them they didn't even need to come cheer me on. All I got in return were road blocks. My mother's resentment and contempt for me increased as time went on. She strangled any love for life I had left with each rejection. My father let her continue to do it. There was never once a win for me. There was nothing left to live for. I realized no matter what I did nothing would ever be right again in my life. That was when I finally gave up asking.

There were many times I laid in my room and thought about suicide. I tried to figure out the perfect plan in my mind so I wouldn't leave any evidence. I was still trying to live within my parents' rules and could not find an acceptable way to end my life. I needed to find a way that would allow people to think everything was fine in our family even after I died. I felt so much grief and deprivation without reprieve. Life had worn my once beautiful, loving, and happy mother down. Years of bitterness stole her joy. She was haggard in misery and she poisoned anyone who tried to help her and her family.

When I got older, I went to summer camp with the other teenage girls my age at church. Even there, I had to put on an act that everything was great in my life. I felt I had to appear to be the best at everything but at the same time not win anything important. I couldn't do anything that might cause me to have to travel anywhere. I couldn't get recognition for anything that would put my parents out in any possible way.

I had to be so observant of everything around me to maintain the status that everything was perfect in our life. I could not appear to rely on anyone. This skill ensured I could help the leaders get us all out of the mountains when they got us lost on hikes a few times. I had to appear wise and clever and make people laugh. I couldn't seem afraid of everything, even though I felt terrified all the time. No one could guess or even think about asking if everything was all right. If they asked deeper questions and tried to find out if I was okay, I would break into a million pieces. I knew they would never be able to put me back together again. We couldn't have *that* now could we? I had to keep people the right amount of distance away to protect the glass castle that they expected me to build. There was no end in sight, and so I could not fall to pieces but had to continue building the glass façade.

I had to pick up the slack on all my siblings' chores when they didn't want to do them, which was often. I'm not saying they didn't do a good enough job and someone had to come behind them and finish. They wouldn't do them *at all*. The chores would sit for weeks and pile up to the point that my parents couldn't take it anymore. The living conditions would become intolerable by anyone's standards.

My parents allowed my siblings' behavior without consequence, and it got worse. If I didn't catch up everyone's chores, my father would beat me. I almost never saw my own parents do any of the catch-up work themselves. They almost never came in to help me. My parents knew they could compel me, and I would obey. I tried fighting back on the dishes when they got very piled up as our family was so large. Dishes that sat for a week or even two got disgusting. We had no gloves, only bare hands. My siblings didn't feel like dealing with chores and didn't care if I did either.

I was not treated like an equal member of the family. First, there was the unfair division of participation in outside activities which didn't account for the uneven workload. To add insult to injury, I would have to remind my parents about someone's birthday. This would not be a big deal under normal circumstances, and it didn't happen too often at first as we were all on the calendar. I helped remind my parents too. As the other kids got old enough to remember their birthdays and read the calendar, they would help too. Then one year my parents forgot my birthday even though I reminded them. As time went on mine was the only one they were not celebrating at all. It wasn't because I was too old now. I asked.

One year I reminded them a hundred times about my birthday for about five or six months even after it had passed. I finally gave up on anything happening for me that year. I didn't even get a cake or a single card that year. They didn't even tell me "Happy Birthday." That was the first year they forgot my birthday for two years in a row. No one wished me a happy birthday the second year either. There was never an explanation given. They never missed anyone else's birthday. They at least made a cake and had a few gifts for the person. I felt like doing that to me two years in a row said something about how they all felt about me. Even after that, anything they did for me they did with great reluctance. They seemed to look forward to everyone else's birthdays and dreaded mine.

I always helped, as required, to get the house cleaned up. I had to get the other kids involved in cleaning and decorating for their parties. It was my job to help my mom so the house would be presentable for a few guests to come by. It was the only time anyone could come over. Over the years, life got worse as the other kids got older. When my birthday rolled around, no one would help clean or decorate, but they did for each other's parties. They told me not to bother them with mine. They were not going to help even if they got spanked.

When that kind of thing happens over and over for years, it takes a huge toll on your self-esteem. The straw that breaks the camel's back is often very small. I have hated my birthday ever since, but I haven't acted out against my siblings for what they did to me. Most people love their birthdays and can't understand how I feel so much vehemence about them. Try and imagine: how horrible would things have to get to make you hate your own birthday? When people mention birthdays, I get this terrible knot inside the pit of my stomach. My strength floods out of my body. I imagine all the things I would like to do to birthdays. But that would never do; we *must* keep up appearances.

I've learned later in adulthood that I can celebrate my own birth by myself. I do anything I want to do all by myself; all-by-myself. That way, there is no room for disappointments, no one to have to please but myself. I can spend the whole day enjoying and celebrating my own life. I have actually had some pretty wonderful birthdays that way. I still feel the struggle inside, though, when that time of the year comes around. I don't know which side will win out: the hermit or the celebrator.

Each year, I can't help but wonder if any of my family will call or send a card. Will they even send an email, something that takes hardly any effort or thought and no expense? Will they send any kind of acknowledgment? They have some accumulated years to make up to me if they want to. Part of me wants them to do it; I hope they prove my inner child wrong, that they prove they do love me. I want them to feel sorry and apologize. Part of me hopes that they *don't* do it so I can have a reason to feel justified in my pain. Still, I want them to feel how awful they were. I hope that they do reach out. I would love for them to prove me wrong.

To show me that the world is a place full of hope and love and joy again. That it is a safe place.

There were sibling rivalries, and then there was the abuse within our own home. I grew up with a sibling who, starting at a very young age, became abusive to everyone in our family. This sibling went out of his way to make it difficult for me to tend and care for the other children. It didn't matter if we were home or farmed out. It was difficult and embarrassing to try and explain things to the parents who watched over us. We didn't know why this sibling was that way. There was a never-ending barrage of horrible things done to the others too. As things worsened with age, my need to try to protect the other children increased. The adults hadn't discovered what was wrong. It was decades until psychologists discovered the dangerous disorders my brother likely had.

Things got so bad for everyone our parents considered giving this child up to the foster care system. They had tried everything known to them to get him to be obedient and kind. Nothing worked. This willful, hate-filled child was out of control. He was destroying every person in our family. And yet he was such a good liar that everyone else thought he was amazing. What they didn't see was that everyone was falling on all sides, casualties to this evil child. I don't think anyone even knew because no one ever did anything about it. This abusive child was even given special privileges over all the other children. It made the cuts sting that much deeper. None of the abuse got reported and charges were never pressed. Back then, you didn't do things like that. It wasn't allowed. We were the Jones family. People might find out we had problems, so nothing got handled.

Our parents were either like zombies (when they were home) or they were gone all the time. They were busy at the hospital, work, or school. There were no examples of healthy relationships in the home. There was only emotional destitution and desperation. When I reported the abuses that I was aware of going on in the home to my parents they did nothing about it. The family was falling apart and no one seemed to notice. The extra privileges the abuser received made dealing with the abuse more difficult. It also encouraged him to be more abusive too, because he got rewarded for bad behavior.

I remember when my parents each pulled me aside to have a discussion with me. They wanted to know what I thought about sending this problem child to foster care. I felt jubilant at first! Then I felt confused and then amazed and betrayed that they would talk to one of their children about adult issues. I felt violated. It is unhealthy to talk to a child about adult issues; it is so inappropriate. It damages children's emotions and trust in adults. Seek professional help and guidance or talk to another adult about your problems. Kids have enough to deal with in life than having an adult put things on them they can't even begin to understand.

I understood the potential consequences of sending the child to foster care. It would be my parents' last hope of saving the family from complete destruction. They must have known my bias. I suppose in some ways they saw me as another adult in the family who couldn't pay rent. I had good insight, but they must have felt unsure of themselves. It may have been they wanted someone else to blame if things didn't work out. I know they felt they had nowhere else to turn. An ignorant professional counselor told them this child couldn't have problems: he was "too young." Our small town did not have access to good counselors. I thought of the phrase, "sacrificing a bad apple to save the rest of the bushel." I knew it would be everything I had been praying for to send this brother away. But with great reluctance I had to suggest that whoever got the child would be in the same danger we faced. Then there would be *two* families damaged by the child's actions and choices.

I didn't want to be their deciding vote. I didn't want to carry any of the blame that might come from any decisions made. I *especially* did not want to be on the receiving end of my brother's wrath if he found out. I left them with my thoughts and their decision-making. They ended up choosing to keep that child in the family and it was an extremely grievous life to be borne. As the years went by, the abusive behaviors and the stress levels continued to increase. We all still smiled and acted as though nothing was wrong in the Jones family. Every day I prayed mightily for deliverance.

We moved right after my parents found out about my sister's cancer. We used to live in a nice neighborhood with lots of great kids. The neighborhood we moved to seemed very different.

We had to deal with bullies now harassing us all the time. I was very lonely in that house. I learned to play with the nicer kids, but I missed my little girlfriend who moved away to another country when we were toddlers. I never got over it for a long time. It scared me to try to make any new friends. I was afraid they would move away without saying goodbye. All that we had left was for all us siblings to play together in our fenced in front yard with the neighbor kids. That was our social life now.

Dad tried to keep the grass mowed for us and he and I got a few greenhouses started. I felt so disconnected from him after they diagnosed my sister with a terminal cancer. I would do anything to spend time with him hoping to restore our relationship. I held wrenches while he worked on the car. I helped with yard work and read all the books on engineering from the library. I hoped we could talk about the things he enjoyed, and things would go back to the way they were. Sometimes we talked about his job. During brief moments, I felt like we had a little bit of a conversation, but it was never the connection we had before.

He once told me he thought of me more like a co-worker: someone he was glad to have there, helping him with the work. He thought of me more as a peer than his offspring. He meant it as a compliment, but it broke my little heart - I wanted my daddy back. After all, you aren't close to your co-workers, and you definitely don't love them or take care of them.

I hated being in the house. Mom always tried to make me stay inside. I felt trapped in there as much as if I had been in any prison. I needed time to be away from my life and the hell that was our house, but I wasn't allowed to leave. If I hadn't known what life was like before the cancer, I might have thought it was normal. I *did* know, though. I couldn't get far enough away from our new house. I couldn't get far enough away from our new *life*. It felt more like death and dying every day. The farther away I was from home, the freer I felt. I hated coming home. I used to wish my parents would send me to foster care.

I never went to any of my school dances as a result of the cancer. Mom turned me down so much for anything that I wanted to do. She did it all the time, so I quit trying to ask for money to go to a movie with my friends or do anything else fun. It wasn't worth the harassment. Over exaggerated sighs and glaring glances from my mother made her message clear. How dare I ask for what had been promised me, that they said I had a right to ask for, on occasion?

My parents told in a private meeting that they couldn't afford to give me an allowance. They weren't going to do this for the other kids. They knew they expected a lot of me because I was older. If there was anything I needed or wanted - like going to the movies with my friends, they told me, to ask. They would try to give me a little money. They wouldn't be able to afford it often, but, if at all possible, they promised me they'd try. If they couldn't, they agreed to let me know they couldn't then. When the situation changed again, they would tell me. If I abused the privilege, it would be taken away. Knowing this was such a sacrifice, I only asked two or three times.

The girls in the family were not allowed to engage in any extracurricular activities. Our parents forced us all to smile and cheer on our brothers and attend and support all their events. We had to go to every single event they participated in - any and every thing that they wanted to do. Anything we girls wanted to do was beat out of us with strong emotional abuse by our mother. How dare we even think about wanting to do anything for ourselves! They taught us in theory that we should have the same equal opportunities as our brothers, but in practice we did not. Hypocrites and liars!

They should have been honest with us from the beginning. They should have told us girls are not allowed to do anything but stay in the house and cook and clean. At least then we would have had the expectation we would have and be nothing more than that - worthless in their eyes. *I* was not worthless.

I hardly ever asked to do anything in the first place. I knew we were in a very tight financial situation due to many expensive doctor bills. I realized how different our life was now compared to before the cancer. I had also become accustomed to not going to do anything with friends outside of school. I made the mistake one time of asking for money to go to a movie dutch treat with a gal from school. My mom reamed me for daring to even ask. After a few extremely negative experiences like that, I swore I never would ask again. My mother was a liar about my parents' promise and made me feel so horrible for even thinking to ask. After I graduated from high school, I would be able to get my own job, I told myself. No one could ever tell me I couldn't go do things I wanted ever again.

I was not allowed to work for money while I lived at home. I had to wait until I graduated high school to get a job. Then, I bought my own car for $500 and sometimes had money to do things. In high school, my mother volunteered me to babysit for free for people she knew. I was never allowed to ask for money and I was exhausted from taking care of her children every day. If I was lucky, someone might give me a couple dollars for a night's work. I wouldn't have minded if it had been my own decision, but I was never allowed to make any of my own choices. It made me feel unworthy of having money or doing things that made me happy. I was glad I could help those families. I knew times were tight for everyone. I wanted a little self-respect and appreciation for some of the work I did.

A couple of times, schoolmates asked what I would do if a boy asked me to a dance. I had to come up with all these reasons why it would be impossible for me to go. I would be babysitting my siblings, or my parents might have to take my sister to the hospital. We might be gone to someone's house or something else very inconvenient.

The cold hard truth was I also didn't want to have to ask my mom. I knew from experience she would say no without regard. It seemed like she resented me. I must have reminded her too much of our life before. That she wasn't keeping her word to me. The only time she wanted me around was to babysit, clean her house, or act as her psychiatrist. She felt like she had no friends because she kept everyone away. I would have liked to experience the rites of passage of youth. My mother checked out of our present reality most of the time. I didn't recognize her anymore.

The only activities that my mom let (read: made) me do were to go to church and be in the school choir. Her mother had done the same to her as a child she said and she hated it, but it made no sense to me why she would then do the same to me. I had no desire for music. I wanted to move, I wanted to run, and I wanted to be in sports. I needed to release all that stress! Every day that I was in school I hated her for resenting me so much. I hated her for making me be in choir and for not supporting *my* dreams or interests. I hated her for so many things and always putting my sister first.

My parents taught me one way but in reality made me live another. That hatred transferred from my parents, fueled the guilt I felt towards my sister, and turned to rage. There was no one appropriate to take my anger out on. There was nowhere for my feelings to go. How could I be angry?

My mother stayed up all night rocking and clinging to her dying child. Some nights she cried in the dark as she rocked death on her shoulder. She could smell the copper in the blood trickling down her back and into her robe. Mom rocked her child alone, scared and devastated. She prayed all night this frail child lived one more hour and another and another until daylight came. She held the delicate, fragile chemo frame of her once cherub-like baby and rocked so our dad could sleep. He had to go to work and school, or he was looking for work because the economy crashed so hard.

A bunch of us shared a room. I'd often see that bald, shiny, alien-like head silhouetted in the door frame of our darkened doorway. The hall light was often still on. My sister lost every bit of hair on her body. It scared me that something could do that to a person. She had no eyelashes, no eyebrows, and no hair. Sometimes I felt angry, and sometimes I thought she looked kind of comical. Often, I felt both at the same time.

Dad was out of work for several long stretches, one time almost a year straight. The economy flopped three different times. He had some good, high paying skills that would have done well in a big city. We had moved to be closer to family after we found out about the cancer. There weren't a lot of places that offered the kind of work our dad could do. We had no food, no money, and for some reason we couldn't even get help from welfare. We needed something to help us get by until he found work. We had family, but none that could help us. Dad did his best to find odd jobs in the meantime. They paid enough to buy a little bit of food and nothing more. They were enough to keep us from receiving any welfare help we needed so much.

I understand why people have strong contempt for those who lie and abuse the welfare system. This man raised us, worked so hard, and gave everything that he could to take care of us. He came home so angry once that he could hardly speak for some time. He finally told us of a lady at the unemployment office who was very obviously lying on her application. She arrived at least an hour or two after he did and sat down right next to him. He could see everything she wrote down on her form. He said she was making up names and putting down fake social security numbers. The socials didn't even have the right number of digits.

He was completely disgusted at her obvious and blatant fraud. He felt sure they would catch her in her deception. He waited for hours trying to find out if he could get some help from welfare: only food for our family, nothing else. They called in the unclean, unkempt woman who had lied on her forms. Not long after - and much to my father's surprise, this woman got a bunch of food stamps and other cash benefits. She left with a smug look on her face. Father thought to himself "If they helped her and didn't penalize her for lying, they will *definitely* help me." It actually gave him hope, which he needed at that point.

Father told how he watched a room full of people who had gotten there long after he had (and the lying woman), come and go. It was almost closing time, and they still hadn't called him back. He was becoming impatient and quite perplexed about why they hadn't called him up yet. He asked a couple of times as the hours rolled by if they had forgotten him or if they were ready for him yet. He needed to be out applying for jobs and trying to get interviews if possible. Why hadn't they called him back to speak with someone? They kept telling him that the case worker wasn't ready for him. Sit and wait and someone would be with him soon.

When the case worker finally *did* call him back, she was in tears. She could hardly speak to my father, and when she did, it was in a shaky whisper. She couldn't even make eye contact with him. She told him that she could not give him the food stamps even though she knew he was honest. She knew he should qualify for them and really needed them more than anyone. When he brought it to her attention, she admitted that she knew that other lady had lied on her forms. She said there was nothing she could do about it.

He told her he knew that they had given the lady food stamps and she didn't deserve them. She agreed. That had made it all the more difficult to tell him he didn't qualify. He was short by one month of being out of work. The case worker admitted she had made him wait so long because she hadn't had the guts to tell him. His tax return from the previous year was too much money and not enough time had passed unemployed. She'd been trying to work up her nerve to tell him the whole day.

He felt this woman had an awful *lot* of nerve. She disrespected him by making him wait so long to tell him he didn't qualify. He was angrier that she had wasted so much of his time. He could have been trying to find a way to make ends meet for his family that day. So many precious hours wasted for nothing! We all were too scared to say anything after hearing that story.

We didn't have a TV for most of my life growing up, at least not once the cancer years started. We didn't go out to eat hardly ever because it cost too much to take everyone. We didn't go out anywhere for the same reason. We didn't spend money on anything! I don't know how we would have survived that year of unemployment if it hadn't been for the generosity of the farmers. They allowed us to glean produce off their land. It allowed us to set aside a little bit of food to save for emergencies, like our wheat grain. Neighbors who were broke themselves came up with odd jobs to help us. I'm sure some of the neighbors got creative making up things for him to do, but he never took a handout, and we were proud of him for that.

The year Dad was out of work, we ate fresh ground whole wheat pancakes made from scratch every morning. We ground the wheat ourselves each day. We topped the pancakes with homemade fruit syrups from the fruit we picked ourselves. There was always the other option of maple flavored syrup. We made it from sugar, water, and maple flavoring. We pureed the fruit and stored it in baggies in our big freezer until we needed it. Then, we heated up the fruit in a pan, added some sugar to taste, and cooked it until dissolved. Mid-day we ate school lunch, and we made sure we ate it all, except for the cooked spinach with vinegar. (Nobody ate the cooked spinach. It didn't matter how hungry you were.) For dinner every night, we ate a stew of potatoes, carrots, and onions we had collected from gleaning.

I remember often feeling terrified that we were going to lose the house. My parents talked

Page 36

about it with me from time to time when they worried it might happen. They told me never to tell the other kids. Knowing we would be homeless people like I would hear about all the time was the scariest thing I could think of. How would we hide *that* from the kids at school and church; would they still let us attend school?

I knew that was not a desirable situation in which to be, no matter whose perspective you looked at it from. I knew the kids at school would be crueler than ever. The kids from church would be the first ones to tell the other kids at school. People loved gossip and didn't care who it hurt when they spread it around. Something bad is happening to someone; let's all talk about it for entertainment! It was bad enough to think we could only afford the barest of necessities for food. To know we were so bad off that we couldn't have a house either anymore was almost more than I could bear.

My parents had it down to the penny exactly what it cost to feed us kids. Every day we had fresh ground, homemade pancakes with syrup made from gleaned fruit. We always got permission where we gleaned beforehand, so we never stole. There was no cheaper way to feed us than what they were doing. They were feeding us on a few pennies per meal per day. Dinner was a little bit more, fifty cents per kid or something. I remember the destitution that those pennies each represented. They even had a friend who did accounting look at the books once to see if they were somehow missing something. He couldn't find any other corners to cut that they hadn't already cut themselves. It surprised him, in fact, how creative my parents were. They found things to do he would never have even thought of.

The year Dad was out of work, we gleaned potatoes, carrots, and yellow onions from some farmers' fields. We put them into our storage shed to keep through the winter. We were so poor we had nothing else to eat aside from some meat the church gave us. That was only meant to tide us over for a short spell. It was stew every night for dinner almost that whole year. Dad had the grain that we used for our breakfast pancakes. Then our mom would make us stew for dinner out of those gleaned vegetables. There were a lot of days we had stew with no meat. We couldn't afford steak for sure; there were too many mouths to feed even if we'd had more money and fewer problems. We usually had ground beef or chicken in the stew, if anything. We always had those same carrots, potatoes, and onions for dinner. We didn't know how long they were going to have to last us. It was better that we didn't know beforehand.

Mom got pretty creative at trying to make those stews taste a little different from time to time. You can only make stew so many ways with so few ingredients and hardly more seasonings than salt and pepper. A couple of times that year, though, we had a little barbecue sauce to add.

I remember going in the kitchen one day several months into eating stew every night. Mom's back wracked in silent torment, and she sobbed silently into her hands. She was half bent over the stove next to the stew pot because all she had to give us to eat was the same stew again. I'd never seen her like that. She didn't want me to see her when she realized I'd come in, and she turned to hide. There was nowhere to go in that tiny kitchen, and I held onto her tight and let her cry for a bit. It would never do for the other kids to find her like that, and she needed to get it out of her system. I wasn't going to let her go through that alone.

When things are so difficult in life, no one should ever have to be alone if it can be helped. I guess even Christ was alone in the Garden of Gethsemane during his greatest adversity (Mark 14:32-50). It must have seemed like eternity to him at the time. No one knows you are struggling if you don't let people know, and you can't expect people to know out of thin air what you need.

If my mom had let people in to be her friend, she could have had an easier time. I could tell after a bit, she felt strengthened by my support. She realized I wasn't going anywhere. She was not alone in the battle of the stew any longer.

As soon as I felt she was ready to go again, I pitched in to help finish making what seemed to be the thousandth pot of stew. I told her to go wash her face and I would finish cooking. She was so tired of stew, she told me. To be honest, I was too. She told me she was even more tired of only being able to give us stew again and nothing but stew with no end in sight. I told her that we had been eating a lot of stew and sometimes it gets old but I really liked her stew. She made a good stew that anyone would be proud to eat. Well, except for one of my siblings who always complained about everything we ate no matter what it was. I told her that didn't count because he never liked anything anyways.

We all ate that stew every night for almost a whole year straight, and we survived. That was the only time I saw Mom lose it like that. She may have cried in the shower or in her room with the doors closed so we wouldn't hear her. She must have cried at Grandma's house when they forced us outside to play while they talked. That time in the kitchen was the only time I ever saw it happen myself.

It wasn't all bad all the time. I learned to overcome a lot of difficulties. I learned a lot about myself, my needs, and others needs too. I learned to *survive* - I'm as tough as nails. I can do anything I want to do, and I care about people in an authentic way and want to help them. I can also eat stew every day for almost a year. I learned to appreciate music. There are a lot of people that are more musical than I am, but I learned an appreciation and enthusiasm for it. I've learned that I still have time as an adult to make all my dreams come true. I can realize things I couldn't do when I was growing up. The only thing that can hold me back is *me*.

I have learned that there are a lot of ways to look at almost everything. There's always another option to reach your goals. I learned there are a lot of deeper layers to people than what they present to you. They are much kinder and loving than you think. Most especially, they deserve our love and understanding more than we know, no matter what. Don't put yourself in danger. Use common sense. But we can all be kinder and extend greater consideration to one another.

I've learned that people usually do things because they are trying to get a love need met. A lot of times we don't know how to communicate that need to each other. Often, we are not even aware what is going on in the first place. That is, until we are able to take a step back and be honest with ourselves. We had examples of this all around us growing up.

Sometimes school kids were mean. They made fun of our clothes that were clean but not stylish. Or they'd be mean to the people we hung out with at school. Our friends had the kindest hearts but the kids judged by outward standards. We had to defend each other at bus stops and on the bus. Kids put gum in our notebook pages, and called us names. The pranks were not too big of a deal except each page of paper was a hardship for our parents to provide to us children.

That was nothing compared to what the adults did, though.

The worst thing people did that was so devastating was after my sister's hair started to fall out in clumps. She had gotten so thin and poisoned from the chemo that she looked like a little anorexic baby. On top of her bones sticking out through her skin she had dark black and purple circles under her eyes. This was because her kidneys were having problems from the treatments. She looked terrible almost all the time. People looked at us like we were horrible, awful people. They walked away from us - and at times even ran. They acted like we were locking her in a cellar with no food and abusing her. They thought she had the plague or something. They feared we were going to throw them and their children in a dungeon and do the same to them.

Kids asked their parents why that girl had no hair and no eyelashes. They asked why she was so skinny, or what was wrong with that girl. People shushed their kids and dragged them to the other side of the street by one arm. They made such a huge scene that soon everyone within earshot would stare at us. They went far out of their way to take a different aisle in the grocery store to get away when they saw us with her. They scurried away, yanking their kids along behind them as fast as they could go.

Mom tried to talk to the ones that were close enough to us. She'd squat down to the kids' levels and explained in a kind and gentle way to them that her daughter had a sickness. It was growing a cancer in her body, and it wasn't anything that anyone could catch from her. The parents usually relaxed a little at this statement but were still horrified. She told them the medicine the doctors had to give my sister to kill the cancer was a poison. The medicine made all her hair fall out and her eyes to have dark circles. She told them that after my sister finished the medicine, her hair would grow back. Then she would look like everyone else, and we hoped she would be healthy and strong again.

This seemed to put everyone at ease when she finished, including the eavesdroppers. We saw some mothers' eyes change from terror, extreme prejudice, and vengeance to sorrow. They felt ashamed they had made a false assumption of the worst kind about our family. They didn't even know us and we turned out to be nice people going through an unimaginably rough time. It could've been *them*, after all.

We did our best to overcome the prejudices and ignorance of people by educating them when we could. We followed Mother's brave and desperate example. It was very difficult for us all.

The time came for my sister to enter kindergarten, but her immune system was barely strong enough. Mom and I went with my sister down to my sister's class the first day. Mom wanted to explain to the kids with their teacher what their new classmate had been through. Mom and the teacher would explain to the kids why she had no hair before she came into the room. Mom let everyone know that my sister needed everyone to help take care of and protect her. She wasn't as strong as they were. Their new classmate would need them to be her special friends.

It hurt to see so many false judgments in the world everywhere we went. It only reminded us how alone we were in this world the way people treated us generally. But, we saw small sparks of hope with each person who listened to my sister's story. This was to be one of those days. I had been waiting outside the classroom door, holding my sister's hand while we waited until it was time. We didn't want her to be alone outside. Mom then told us it was time to enter the room full of waiting children. They all strained to catch the first glimpse from the carpet squares on the floor as they stood up. They sat as they listened to the instructions. As we entered the room, the beautiful children rushed to my sister with love, hugs, and acceptance. The room filled with joyful welcomes and hellos.

After that, my sister often returned from school exhausted. She'd throw herself onto the nearest furniture and drape her hand across her forehead. She'd then proceed to complain about how she had too many friends. In a twist of irony, I felt I had none. I always had to be available to maintain balance in our home and fill in the gaps. Our parents didn't want the other children to feel as much of the stress. I couldn't afford to be close to anyone.

I don't think I would have made it to adulthood if I had not read scriptures as much as I did. I had my very own copy to read. I didn't have access to bodywork back then to help, though. My whole family could have used it. I did not feel that God was listening to me or helping me at that time in my life. I didn't understand the nature of God and his plan, especially for me. I felt so dead inside all the time. God was my escape. It gave me hope there were better days to be had *someday*, and that someday God might be real. I wanted to strive for the best within my ability with what I had to work with. I had hope God would release me from this captivity like Joseph of Egypt. His half-brothers hated him and threw him into a pit to kill him and instead sold him as a slave. Many years later, God delivered him, after he was set up to deliver his whole family from the famine in Egypt.

Like Joseph, my brothers hated me, but I was less trusting of God than Joseph. I felt from time to time there might be a God but couldn't understand why he wasn't helping me. God does things in his own time and in his own way, and he wasn't doing them in *my* time or way despite my prayers, now. He wasn't doing them in the way I asked him to do. I forgot to account for the fact that God allows all people the agency to act according to our consciences or not. He may have been trying to send me help. It is possible people weren't listening or were but chose not to act. I'll never know.

The biggest factor is that God is playing for the end game, not the temporary here and now. His healing will be complete and full.

The doctors diagnosed my sister with a terminal illness so no one wanted to help or touch her with a ten-foot pole. The stress and devastation of the medical bills piled up in the millions. As doctors tried to figure out what to do with this never-before-seen rare cancer, it got to be very expensive. Due to the bad economy and being out of work so much, we often did not have health insurance. We had nowhere to turn for help. There was no way we would ever be able to pay off the bills during our lifetime. We kids would have to plan to pick up paying them off once our parents died, and then *our* kids too. The cancer groups said they'd help; that was, unless you're dying. Where do you go when no one wants to help you, and they can't make money off of you anymore because you may die soon?

We knew what the woman with the blood issue in the Bible must have felt like. She'd spent her life savings on doctors who could never cure her. My parents went to every single charitable organization they could find too. They asked for any kind of help they could get for their dying daughter. Our situation was very dire, and we thought *we* would die from the strain and lack of support. No one would help us.

After much searching, my parents finally found one group. It's a very large, well-known company that you would definitely recognize if I gave you the name. They said they would help my parents and put $1000 into a trust fund for each year that my sister survived. She could only use it for college if she lived past eighteen years old. At that time, she would receive it at her college of choice. If she didn't survive, the expenses could go towards her burial and nothing more. Any remaining money would then return to the company. We were so grateful and it was more than we had hoped for!

Things changed when my sister survived longer than they wanted or expected her to. This foundation of *hope* and *promise* quit putting money into an account for her. It had been seven years in the making. They got real busy looking for a loophole to get out of their deal. They didn't want to pay anything more. They came up with some obscure loophole that they had to twist into next year to make fit their purpose. They not only quit paying money into the trust fund, they also took all the money away that they had already given.

It left my family with nothing to hold onto. My sister would have nothing to look forward to, nothing to fight for to stay alive. The company ripped everything right out from under us. The trust fund had been the very last thing keeping our family going after all those years. The money in the account was like proof to us all that she might survive. It hinted that someday a miracle would happen. It said she would be able to go to college. The rest of the family knew we would have to spend our lives in slavery until we paid all the medical bills.

When the company that had promised funds to help my sister took them away again, I felt a huge wobble in our family. We'd been hanging on by the skin of our teeth already. We found out the company made the decision to reverse their help without notice. They didn't want us to be able to do anything about it. They had the bank pull all the money out of the account without warning and then sent my parents a letter. It told my parents what they had done. It was in that moment I felt my parents, especially my mother, would fall down dead in front of me. She almost did.

When I got older, I took my mom to see a special doctor who did some tests on her. He said he didn't know how she got herself there or how she was even alive. I had forced her to go and had driven her there myself because I knew something was wrong. Grandma was dead and couldn't help her anymore. Mom was so messed up health-wise that she started sobbing uncontrollably. She had to answer the question on the intake form that asked, "Why are you here today?" She didn't know what to put down. Then, she couldn't even answer any of the other questions after her name.

Where was the morality that this company claimed they had? They had promised to help my sister, and then they took everything away. If they could only see what they had done to my mother, they might have been sorry.

I had sacrificed every part of who I was, who I wanted to be, all my hopes and dreams. I united with my parents in a family effort to get this one person out of the family alive. My sister would be the miracle child. She would have a mighty work to do.

It was too much for my family. They watched over this young toddler sleeping in that first hospital bed. We knew she might die any minute. We felt the consequences looming over us like a tsunami waiting to destroy us. It was difficult for my parents, as they thought about losing such a beloved child. It was difficult for me fearing my sister would live. I feared I would never be happy, safe, or joyful ever again.

My parents finally came to terms with the impending death of my sister. They were willing to accept God's will, whatever it was. They were expecting and prepared in every way for her to die. I watched my whole family follow their example of acceptance of what was to come. I followed suit though my reasons might have been different at the time. You'd never find another family more at peace about something like this. It was very difficult for everyone when things did not go as we thought God had planned. You would think that it would be a happy, joyful thing to rejoice, to have a loved one destined to die who now wasn't, especially in someone so young with life unlived. We asked God:

"Wait, what? But we were willing to accept that she was going to die. We are ready and prepared to accept your will."

Nice sense of humor, God, nice play. It's easy to go along with what you're prepared to go along with, but that's not the part that God wanted from us. He wanted a part of me and my family that we didn't even know was ours to give. We all have a part we are holding back. We hold it back from others, even from ourselves. We hold it back from letting go of the things that are hurting us.

I worked a lot, and I made progress that changed my life.

I have found that the massage work that I have received has had an incredible healing effect. Over time, I have learned to let things go. It has let me see how much God truly loves me and cares about me and every single one of us. He was there with me, but I was so consumed by my own guilt and anger that I could not see or feel his influence in my life. I didn't understand it before but He is ever so wise and gives us the tools to find the way to him if we ask for his help. Usually, it takes a lot of time and effort on our part to see the final picture and/or rewards. We can't ever give up on the process. It's not just given to us. We have to work for it. God said he gave us work to be a blessing to us. I can see that is true now.

Along my journey, I have tried to get to know God better and tried to follow his example. It's also helped me to get massage on a regular basis, at least once a month, to meet my healthy touch needs. My family didn't hug much to show affection growing up. That was difficult for me but now I know what to do.

Therapeutic massage taught me that healthy and appropriate touch is important. It helped me establish good personal boundaries. I learned that massage is a very essential need for the organs of the body and systems. Sometimes they need help to clean out all the physical, spiritual, and emotional junk. Acupressure treatments helped balance my organs and emotions. Cranial Sacral Therapy helped with a few head injuries that I had received. It also helped release some long-trapped emotions. I've felt so much better since then.

I had some amazing experiences that opened my heart back up a lot. I was able to release a lot of emotional trauma that had built up. It happened quicker than I ever could have done in counseling sessions, and it was much gentler. I have felt life coming back into my soul again for the first time since I was a child. Essential oils have also been of great benefit to me too from time to time as I have needed different things. That surprised me quite a bit.

Over my own life God had helped me in his time to heal with the help of bodywork. I have learned to appreciate my sister. In spite of the many different challenges we faced growing up we have been there for each other. I don't know if God's purpose in keeping her around was so I could have a change of heart. It now seems like a lifetime ago - that day as a very young child, next to a hospital bed, on a hard plastic chair. I don't know if he has other reasons in store but I now find myself on the other side of the scale about my sister's life.

I find myself pondering each day on the dreams that I have had about the end of my life. I remember the dreams about the end of my sister's life. The stories she told me about when and how her departure from life will come. I find now I am more and more anxious about how I could possibly go on without her being a part of mine. I have a feeling that each day I am running out of time to spend with her, to laugh with her, to cry with her. I dread the day that the Lord will call to take her home and I will be left here without her companionship. She is my sister, my partner in crime, my best friend.

Chapter 2
Broken

WHEN WE WERE YOUNG, our dad challenged us to do difficult things for fun. He was trying to wear us out. It became quite a game to us and we looked forward to and enjoyed each new challenge to overcome with our bodies. There were things we never thought of doing before. Could we roll our tongues up like a straw? Could we spread our toes apart? Then, could we move each toe by itself and separate from the others? What about shape our fingers into a Vulcan hand greeting like Mr. Spock played by Leonard Nimoy on *Star Trek*? Could we do Nano-Nano fingers like Mork from the show *Mork and Mindy* that starred Robin Williams?

Our favorite challenge was learning to cross our eyes. Trying to make wall-eyes is very difficult to do if you haven't ever tried it. For those who haven't it's the opposite of crossing your eyes by making them look away from each other at the same time. It was a game of self-discipline, and some of us kids were better at it than others. There were seven of us all together. I doubt any of us at the time thought consciously of applying this same principle to other areas of our lives. It is a simple idea that is easy to apply to anything you like using the same method. Pick something simple to start, begin to focus on the thing you are trying to do and figure out a way to make it happen. As you become more confident, you can then try more difficult things. It is never too late to learn to try new things and new ways of doing and thinking about things. Everyone can benefit from self-discipline.

We always looked for creative ways to one-up one another with the challenges in our household. At times we were a bit like circus monkeys. I imagine the neighbors and even our parents thought so. I hope we brought a little brightness into their lives with our antics. I remember once we were watching TV and there was some show that had a contortionist as one of the acts. They folded themselves all the way up like a little twisty pretzel inside a tiny one-foot square box. You could see through the clear glass box so you could tell they were actually completely inside. Then, they also closed the lid on top so you knew that they were all in there!

They then let the person out of the pretzel box, untwisted themselves back up to standing, and took a deep bow. We, like the audience in the show, we were completely amazed. We sat staring with our mouths hanging open, holding our breaths, not daring to make a sound. My dad was the first to break the stunned silence where time had frozen us. His comment was: it would take a very special person to be able to do something like that. They would have to have extra-long tendons from birth or something along those lines.

I wanted my father to think of me as a very special person, so I spoke up. I had a different idea. That could be true, but if a person did a lot of stretching for long enough, they would become flexible. They could become flexible enough that anyone might be able to do the same thing. He looked at me like he was half-challenging me and half-considering what I suggested. He said, "Oh, you think so, do you?" Challenge accepted. I picked up the gauntlet and told him that I would prove it to him.

When the family piled onto the couch while we watched television, I would be on the floor trying to stretch. While I read my reading assignments and when I read the Bible I would be stretching. This went on for a few years, and I began to succeed in my goal. When I started, I could hardly touch my knees. I was very stiff and inflexible, and I wondered if I had bitten off more than I could chew with this challenge. A twinge of self-doubt started to enter my mind. I immediately squashed the thought, knowing it would not help me reach my goals.

I got to where I was able to do some pretty fantastic things. As I exercised and worked hard on my chores at home, I got stronger and I grew taller. I felt so invincible once I realized that I was strong enough to run up the side of a building like Jackie Chan. I got strong enough to break an apple in half with my bare hands, hardly even touching it. (It's an amazing trick to someone who never has seen anyone do something like that and it became a great party trick.)

I became strong enough by the time I was a teen that my dad taught me a little about the skill of canoeing. He taught me the basics of steering in a rough river but wasn't sure what to expect on this one trip. We attended a group trip and he was the leader of the boating activity. As we climbed into the canoes, he told me that on this trip he would have no other person steer the boat he was in but me. I said he only wanted me in the boat because I was his kid and didn't want me to get hurt. He very firm and told me that was not the reason.

He told me in private, that no one else in the group had the skill level I had developed that he himself had taught me. We were going through some rapids but he didn't know what type, and he wasn't familiar with this river. He didn't want anyone in his boat to get thrown out and crack their heads on a rock or drown. He was very skilled. The responsibility for his passengers' lives was of serious import to him.

He and his best friend once snuck down a class five river rapid that was then closed to the public. Too many people died trying to go down it, but Dad and his best friend made it down. Don't get me wrong, they had a few very close calls. The river had been named after the devil. I don't recall the exact name of the river anymore, but officials had closed it to the public for a reason. Anyone who knows class five rivers knows that you don't go out of your way to go down them. You could die a horrible and terrifying death. He thought years later after he had gotten married and started having kids that they'd been kind of dumb to do it. At the time they wanted to prove how good they were to themselves and they sure did. They never did it again, though.

These years growing up and this challenge I went through that I am about to tell you, changed my life forever. I want you to understand how strong I was and thought I was so that you can see how weak I really was before. See how my weakness made me stronger by the end of the story. To me, this is my life. I know nothing else. I hope you will feel inspired to share my story with someone who may be struggling with their own trials in life. Know you can overcome them.

After I graduated from high school, I ran around with other single people my age, having a great time. I remember when I got asked out on a date by this guy who all the girls thought was so handsome and hoped to go out with. He had a great motorcycle too. He invited me to ride quads with him in the sand dunes that were near our home in California. Of course, I accepted the invitation.

I admitted that I had no experience riding quads. He only had one quad anyway, so I rode behind him for the most part, and he did most of the driving. I was very relieved not to have to suffer the embarrassment of not knowing how to drive a quad. I was very nervous about the date. He was one of the most handsome guys I had gone out with up to that point.

I went and it was fun until we would hit these huge bumps in the dunes, which *sounds* great. The problem was that I was so short and lightweight that I almost flew off the quad every time we went up a hill. With a little bar behind the seat cushion and him not staying positioned there was little to hold onto. Then I came crashing down on top of that metal bar with my tail bone over and over. It was very painful, but I didn't want to say anything and sound like a wimpy girl or he might not ask me out again. So, I kept riding around with him like that until I was turning green from the pain and couldn't take it anymore.

When he got his fill of quadding and I got my fill of the tail bone crushing, we decided it was time for the date to be over. He asked me if I had wanted to go grab some food but I was so nauseated. I couldn't bring myself to tell him what had happened to my tailbone so we ended the date there, and he took me home. He never did ask me out again, and I was actually okay with it.

The day that we had gone quadding was a Thursday during summer vacation. The next day, our big group of friends went up to this amazing mountain cabin that someone had for one day. I ice packed my tail bone and figured it would be fine. I would just have to be a little careful with it until it healed.

We had so much fun at the cabin. We played all kinds of fun and crazy games like Capture the Flag. On a mountain you have to climb over huge fallen trees as tall as I was and giant boulders. It was very adventurous, and I loved every minute of it. I made a lot of new friends pretty fast and was glad that my friend invited me to start coming to things. There were separate sleeping accommodations for the guys and girls. We got to sleep on the concrete floors with our sleeping bags on one level, and the guys were all in the basement. The next day, we headed back home.

There was a huge church picnic and a lot of people from all over our home town would be there.

Because we lived near a small lake, someone always brought their boat and water skis. There was swimming and a ton of barbeque, corn on the cob, watermelon - and of course - my aunt's famous chocolate cake. Aunt Beatrice was famous for her recipe. She was so famous in fact that no one would let her ever make anything else. She was always a little disappointed about that because she was a very good cook and made many other things too.

Grandma's chocolate cake was delicious too, but a little different. Her secret ingredient was pecans. She and Aunt Beatrice always fought for best cake recipes, and the people at church would egg them on. You should have seen the two of them go at it. People went crazy for my grandma's cake. Hers had a little mayo in the batter for moisture. Aunt Beatrice's recipe was a little heavier on the cream but was almost the exact same recipe aside from the pecans. Grandma was a bit of a stinker, I thought; she never did share her recipe with anyone outside of the family. Sometimes the church folks threw a buffalo or something else in a pit and roasted it up, and that was so yummy. There were also games, water sports, and lots of eating and visiting going on.

That particular year, we had a new family move into town. They didn't know anyone except their grandfather, who lived down the street from our grandma. We visited her, befriended them, and helped them get to know the rest of the people at church. We pretty much knew everyone since we lived in that part of town forever. The town was nice.

One of the new family's daughters, Jane, was very close in age to me. She hadn't come camping with us because she had to work. I agreed to meet up with her at the picnic. As soon as we got back from the campout, we all went straight to the park. We were looking forward to having a lot of food to eat. Of course, Aunt Beatrice and Grandma would be going at it with whose cake was the best! I remember I had a great time. When we played volleyball in the grass I dove for the ball and played to win; I was all in.

A big group of my friends decided it was time to go join in on the water skiing and called to me to come and join them. It never interested me to try to learn to water ski; I had a small frame, and I have never been a very strong person. I always knew, somehow, that I would get messed up if I fell and hit the water and not recover very well from it. I always passed it up in favor of something else.

That day, though, because I had spent the last several years working out, I felt the strongest I had ever been in my life. I had been weight lifting and stretching a lot, plus I was much more active than when I was a little kid. Their calling me had a pull for the first time ever to join them and try it out. I felt that my body could handle it, and I could be very successful at it too. I could feel my spirit rising up within me to accept the challenge. I prepared my lungs to call back out to them that I would join them but then I felt a little quiet voice inside of me. It seemed to say in the most noncommittal and nonchalant way "Umm... hmm... no... not today... don't go today..."

The voice was so quiet, peaceful, and calm. It was even an almost relaxed feeling - as if it didn't matter one way or the other. I also remembered at the same time my new friend Jane was completely terrified of water. That would be the perfect out for me to listen to the feeling that came into my mind.

I called out to them I would go with them next time and I was going to stay and keep Jane company instead. She insisted I go and not stay on her account. I told her that I didn't feel like going today and would rather stay and visit with her. I said I felt tired from playing so much volleyball. So we continued on with the rest of the picnic. I don't remember anything else about that day. We stayed until the sun began to go down and then all went home and got ready for bed.

The next day was Sunday and so we went to church. The service was early and we rushed about to get ready. We all liked to sleep in and shower in the morning so there was chaos with only one bathroom. I woke up with the beginnings of a real whopper of a headache.

We were almost running late and so I grabbed a headache remedy. I figured that I got dehydrated from all the activity and, after all, this was summer time. I should have eaten more watermelon or drunk more lemonade or something. I could have gotten twisted around a little bit one of the times I dove for the volleyball. I figured it would work itself out.

We went to church and part way into it I leaned over to my mom and told her I couldn't handle the pain from my headache. It was getting worse. I needed something stronger than regular strength headache medicine. She said there was extra strength out in the car, so I slipped out to grab some.

I try not to use medication unless it's bad and then use the least amount possible. I don't believe it is good for my body to take medicine so I only took one. After thirty more minutes and no relief coming, I took the second extra-strength pill. Over the next two hours, I maxed out the full daily dosage of every type of headache medication you can take. That included migraine medicine.

Nothing brought even the smallest amount of relief - in fact, my headache got worse. I wanted to rip my own head off I was in so much pain. I had migraines in the past and this was a doozy. I went home, locked myself in a dark room, and waited for relief to come.

I waited for it to pass, like migraines usually do. When dinner time came, my dad wanted to check my back and see if I had something out of place. He first checked my neck. I had a displaced vertebra that had been that way as long as I could remember. My parents never took me to the doctor after a car accident when I was younger. We couldn't afford for me to go. Dad looked at it, and didn't recall that about my neck, and said he was pretty sure I had a rotated disk in my neck. He'd heard they were very painful.

He insisted I needed to get in to see a chiropractor first thing in the morning. Mom knew
Page 63

a chiropractor and called to see if it would be possible to get me in first thing in the morning. He was very happy to try and help us out and to come in before his normal business hours. He already had a full day scheduled with clients.

First thing Monday morning, my mom drove me to the chiropractic office. Incapacitated, I curled up in a ball in the back seat with my entire head covered to protect my eyes from the light. There was no way I would have been able to drive myself. We filled out all the required paperwork and then he had me go through a series of range of motion tests. Everything seemed perfect that way. He then said he would like to have me change into a gown so he could take a look at my spine. He said, "We may need to do x-rays as well."

Once I had changed, Dr. Chipson had me sit on this little bench that looked like it doubled as place to do adjustments. He came around behind me to check my neck. Mom sat across the room opposite from me. He started out looking at and feeling along the back of my neck. He was careful and thorough. Sometimes he'd ask if anything hurt at all. I told him about the funny vertebra at the base of my neck there and what had happened. He agreed and said there was nothing out of the ordinary there. It was very common place for people to have that a little out of place for a variety of reasons.

He continued on to say the neck and lower back are like a mirror to each other. Sometimes when one is out, the other will register the pain. He was going to check the rest of my back to see that the other vertebrae were also in their proper places. I agreed that was fine, so he continued down along my spine until he finally said, "Oh. I may have found what's going on here." He called over to mother and asked her to come around. He wanted to show her something about the back that she might not know.

I suspected very much something was wrong the instant he said that he wanted my mom to come over and take a look. I started to twist around to see what was going on and he asked me again to sit still. He tried to tell me nothing was wrong, there was nothing to see. He only wanted to teach my mother something about the back.

I was *sure* he was not telling me the truth and that put me into a state of agitation. I wanted to twist to see even more. He was a very large man, looking a bit more like a lumberjack than a chiropractor, with his big mustache. His hair was stick-straight and he had a lot of it. He insisted I sit still. I started to comply as Mom came around the end of the bench. She looked over to where I'm sure he was gesturing near my back. She gasped in surprise and shock - and a little horror.

I need to explain something here. Mom had never done that before to my knowledge, never made a gasping sound like that. I have never before or since heard her make that sound. She tried to recover her composure, but I had seen her shoot her hand up to her mouth. I heard her gasp that horrible sound. She tried to cover it with a calm and curious sounding "Oh, that's interesting...what is that?" tone in her voice but she couldn't quite cover up the slight tremble as she spoke. I'm sure she had only said that for my benefit and to try and cover up her initial reaction. I was positive now I was going to die. I was definitely resolute in needing to see what was so awful my *mother* had such a surprised reaction. She had been a nurse part time off and on for the hospital for the last fifteen years and had seen a lot of crazy things.

Dr. Chipson said, "I'm pretty sure I know what this is, but I don't want to say anything until I take x-rays and know for sure."

He asked us to step over to the x-ray machine, and we did that. He made the necessary adjustments, took the pictures, and then developed them. He showed the finished x-rays to us and told us what was going on - and it was exactly what he thought.

He said one of the vertebrae in my lower back had broken completely in half. The front part was sliding forward. The back part with all the bumps that stick out to hold it in place was coming out. It was sliding backwards.

We couldn't even comprehend what that meant even though we were looking right at the x-ray. We were in shock. He explained further as he pointed with a pencil on the x-ray that the vertebrae are shaped like a donut with a hole. The spinal cord goes through the hole. The spines on the back of the bone hold them stacked on top of the other vertebrae. You have little nerves that come out all over the place around them. When the bone breaks like this sometimes people get paralyzed right away. It severs the nerves, and then the signal can't get down from the brain to tell the muscles what to do.

My vertebra was still partly on in the front so it hadn't severed the nerves that come out on the sides. The back half of it was coming out of place completely. The body would dissolve it and reuse the calcium elsewhere most likely. If the front piece of the bone slipped off, it would paralyze me for the rest of my life.

My mind reeled. I could see, no mistaking, on the x-ray that what he was saying was true. I was twenty-one years old and, before this, had felt like I was coming into the prime of my life. Now I was being confronted with the very real possibility of never being able to walk again? All I could think to ask was what this meant for me. I needed to know if my life was over as I knew it. I was getting involved in the local city league teams; I was getting really strong. I had recently gotten my own car that I paid for myself and was able to drive all over creation. I had a job I loved, and my social life was right where I wanted it to be.

I felt completely numb as I sat there devastated. My mom and I grabbed each other's hands, and I was glad that she was there with me right at that moment. I don't think I could have handled that news alone. I half heard as he explained it was not a completely hopeless case. He had a butcher for a client who had a similar issue with his back but not quite as bad as mine. They had been able to reduce his vertebrae back into place more. He was carrying around big sides of pork every day, all day long. I wasn't going to be doing anything like *that* now was I? We sort of laughed, and I said no. He explained what he felt was the best option.

The chiropractor told me that surgery would not even be an option when I asked him about it. So many people were suing doctors for botched back surgeries so they weren't doing them anymore. If I did find someone that would do it, I would have to go to New York or somewhere back East. I couldn't believe it! There was no way I would be able to afford a plane ticket back to New York let alone afford having surgery. According to the chiropractor, no one would even do it anyway. We trusted this person; he was a good man. My mom knew him from when they went to school before he had gone on to attend a chiropractic college.

We trusted that what he said was true, and we were in shock. This is exactly why they say to always get a second opinion - I will tell you why in a little while. We believed the chiropractor so much that we started immediately on treatments. As he recommended, I went several times a week. I would do certain exercises that would help to push the bone back into place on my spine. I had exercises to stretch the right muscles and tighten others. I did those exercises like my life depended on it, and it did. I could not bear the thought of going through the rest of my life without being able to walk, let alone run, ever again.

I kept doing my exercises and going to chiropractic appointments for about a year. Finally one day, my dad came home from work quite distraught and, insisted I go to see our family doctor. The guys at work couldn't believe I hadn't even been to see a medical doctor about my back and he couldn't take it anymore. I had decided it was a waste of money and time for the doctor to tell me the same thing our good chiropractor had told us.

Plus, my dad had bills up to his ears and then some and could definitely *not* afford me to see a doctor right now. He said he would pay for it if he had to, to make me go, and see what our family doctor had to say about it. I respected my father too much to not honor his wishes. I told him that I would find a way to pay for it and to go soon.

I made it in to see our doctor and explained my situation and what had happened since then. I asked him if he knew of any surgeons who would be able to talk to me or help me. He said "Oh, yeah," with his accent, pulled out a pad of paper, and immediately wrote down the names and numbers of five back surgeons. Three of them were within our state. I couldn't believe my ears or my eyes! I felt hope welling up inside of me as if I had wings on my feet. At the same time I felt the burning of red-hot betrayal.

The first thing I did when I got home was to call every name on that list. I worried they might tell me what the chiropractor had told me *and* was afraid they wouldn't. Some of the names on the list

I was definitely *not* going to be doing any business with. I didn't like the god complex a lot of them and their front desk people seemed to have. They talked down to me when I had questions for them.

There was one name on the list that I felt good about. Everyone I talked to was very courteous, polite, and helpful at that office. It was also convenient that it happened to be about the closest place on the list too. I called them back after doing some serious praying to help me know I was making the right decision. I scheduled an appointment with them to meet with the doctor to discuss my situation and options.

My appointment was in the morning a little before lunchtime. My mom and I thought that would work out since it was a three-hour drive from where we lived to get to this place. We would be home well before dinner. The doctor was very nice and wanted to take new x-rays. The last ones the chiropractor took were six months old to show my progress. We had brought a copy of the chiropractor's x-rays and the surgeon was very impressed with how clear they were. He said chiropractic x-rays weren't very good quality most of the time.

The surgeon proceeded to have me go through range of motion tests. He was very careful about how far and where I moved while we waited for the x-rays. He documented everything with great care. I had become quite flexible and very strong with my activities. He was very surprised I could even touch my knees let alone farther than that. On every test, I far exceeded a normal person's range.

He got the x-rays, and we sat together as he compared the two sets.

He showed us the chiropractor's diagnosis. It was a range three out of four with four being the worst before your vertebra slips off and it paralyzes you. He also pointed out the treatment's slight improvements on the second x-ray. Chiropractic treatments pushed the bone back only one-eighth of an inch instead of the quarter. Since that time, I had actually lost the good ground that I had made and now I was a grade four; the most dangerous level. I supposed it was due to lifting heavy items at work, counteracting my exercises.

The doctor said that he had good news and bad news for me. He asked which I wanted first, and all ability to think left my brain. I couldn't imagine that there could be worse news than I could be paralyzed for the rest of my life. I couldn't *imagine* hearing worse news than that. How could there be more bad news? The bad news had happened already, last year. I must have been going into shock again. He said, yes, while he did do back surgeries - and a lot of them - this situation was outside of his comfort zone and ability. My back that was considered a grade three-out-of-four grades was now definitely a grade four. That was the bad news. I thought I would die right there in the chair, and I was very glad I was sitting down at that moment. My life as I had known it was about to end in a devastating and permanent way.

The good news was he had a colleague in the same office that was even better at these surgeries than he was. We could schedule an appointment to see him, and he might be able to help us. We asked if we would be able to get in today to see him. He said that would not be possible as his schedule was already booked full and had been for months. We could get an appointment in a few weeks with him due to the nature of my condition, though.

We were devastated. It had been a very expensive trip for us to drive all the way out to this office. It had been very difficult and complicated schedule-wise to orchestrate. It would be an extreme hardship for us to turn around and come back again in a week or two. It seemed our situation might be very urgent now. We suggested we take the good doctor out and buy him lunch and speak with him while he ate. We could wait until the end of the day and have five minutes of his time to look at the x-rays and his notes.

He looked at our strained faces, made a decision, and left us to make a call. He returned with the news we hoped and prayed to hear. The other doctor would take a half lunch and squeeze us in before his next client after he grabbed some food. We prayed and thanked God for helping us out in our great time of need. We thanked him for hearing our prayers to touch the surgeons' hearts to help us.

We went to grab a quick bite to eat ourselves and were there to meet the doctor as soon as he walked up to the building. He moved at a very fast pace. We did not want to waste a second of his precious time and we almost ran to catch up to him. He led us back into the locked-up offices and asked us to follow him after locking the front door behind us. He didn't want anyone to wander in before the secretaries returned from their lunches. He said he looked at my x-rays and chart from the other doctor while he'd had his lunch. He had a little good news for us but to not get our hopes up. He knew the other surgeon said I was now a grade four, but I was only three-and-a-half to three-quarters. I didn't find much consolation in that.

We spoke about all my options. To continue with chiropractic care, surgery, and other things, and included doing nothing. We discussed the consequences of each option available to me. He went over the repercussions for the rest of my life for each as I got older and my body wore out more. He showed me x-rays of other people he'd worked on, most of whom were elderly; but one was a seventeen-year-old gymnast. He showed me the hardware that he would use to stabilize the spine. I would end up being the youngest person he'd ever done the surgery on that wasn't a professional gymnast. We talked about the processes of each and the options. He was very thorough and answered each one of our questions to our full satisfaction.

This kind surgeon was getting very close to his scheduled appointment time and we didn't want to make him late. He told me that my situation was not a life-or-death emergency as far as that was concerned. Still, it was delicate enough that if I opted for surgery, if it were him, he would not wait too much longer. The farther off the pedicle slips, the more difficult the surgery. There was also a greater chance of more nerve damage being permanent. That was even if the surgery went well. We told him we would think and pray about it and get back to him to let him know what we decided to do.

I don't recall if it was before we got out of the office, started down the road and went back, or called after we got home. It wasn't long before I knew I would opt for the surgery. It was the right choice, and Mom felt the very same thing. As active as I liked to be and the way I am I knew if I did not have the surgery I would end up in a wheelchair. I needed to have that bone stabilized. I am so grateful to this day for that surgeon's candor and honesty. He even discussed other options that would not benefit him at all, with frankness. I felt like he was looking out for my best interests. He supported me to make the decision I felt was right for me and not his pocketbook. I called and let them know I was going to go ahead and have the surgery.

They wanted to get started right away. They would need to collect a bunch of my blood over the course of several visits to have on hand for the surgery. They didn't want to use someone else's because the body likes its own blood more than anyone else's. They needed to fit me for a fiberglass back brace cast. Then there was the task of setting all the appointments for everything. They had to make reservations for the operating room, anesthesiologist, and a lot of other things. It surprised me my surgery wouldn't be for three months. I was too light and short to donate my own blood more often, so we had to wait for my body to make more and recover afterward.

The surgeon's team at the office told me I had to quit my job. I was not allowed to even step off a curb because any jarring might cause the bone to slide more. That would cause more nerve damage or even paralysis. I didn't know what to do with myself without a job and so I signed up to take a few college courses in the meantime. It drove me crazy with boredom not being able to do anything anymore. I shouldn't have done that, even with the aid for my condition, but the classes helped pass the time. I had to be careful in the extreme about everything that I did. I saw God's hand helping me through it all.

Month by month I would make the long drive to the town where they'd perform the surgery. I donated my own blood. They wanted to make sure that they had enough of my own blood not to have to use someone else's, and I was grateful for that. I followed all their instructions to a "t," no matter how silly some of the things seemed.

The day of the surgery grew closer, and I had my bag packed. The college semester ended. I made arrangements with everyone I would need help from and asked them to pray for a successful surgery. I did everything that I could think of to prepare my physical, spiritual, and mental self. I'd go over the procedure and possible complications and various outcomes. I got a priesthood blessing to ask God to watch over me and to help me recover well. We asked him to bless the doctor and the team that would be working on me and helping me. We prayed that they would be inspired and that their hands would be guided.

The day came and my surgery was scheduled for before sun up. Mom drove me over to the hospital and I tried to doze on the ride over. She would wait for me to come out of the surgery and stay with me during my recovery. She stayed with some relatives later that night who'd heard she was in town. They expected an hour-and-a-half long procedure then an equal recovery time from the anesthesia.

Once I arrived, they had me change into a hospital gown and went over the checklist one more time. They wanted to be sure I understood everything that would be happening. They wanted to be sure I understood every possible risk and then asked if I still wanted to proceed. They were so competent that I felt very comfortable and at peace that everything would be fine. I had never been under anesthesia, so I was a bit nervous about that. I would be in the hospital for five days in recovery, so I knew it was not going to be a picnic. They gave me a shot to make me fall asleep and told me to start counting backwards nice and slow from one hundred. They told me I wouldn't make it; that most people usually only get to about ten before they fall asleep. I made it to about fifty or so before I lost consciousness.

I don't remember anything after falling asleep until I woke up in my hospital room. Then, it was the strangest experience of my life. I had the hardest time getting my eyes to open up. It was like they were more sticky and heavier than anything I had felt and they wouldn't move when I told them to open. I wondered if they might have taped them shut for the surgery; it felt like I needed a forklift to raise my upper lids. It took several attempts, but then I could see sunlight filling the room. Everything was a white blur of light. I struggled for a few more minutes trying to get my eyelids open even a crack to be able to see where I was. I had no sense of anything else other than my attempting to do that one thing.

Once I finally got enough of a peep through a crack in one eye, I could make out my mom sitting in a chair across the room. It seemed so far away. She was looking at a magazine. I wasn't able to talk or move and I felt like a giant slug lying there. I had a great idea that if I could move my arm at least, then she would know I was awake. I began to focus all my effort into bending my arm at the elbow up towards my head. It was too heavy to try to raise my whole arm.

As I brought it upward, I caught sight of someone moving an arm towards me that I didn't recognize. The arm's movement didn't seem to quite match mine, either. To my shock it looked kind of like Mom's hand. I had a disembodied experience for a second or two in slow motion. I stared at this strange thing floating effortlessly in front of my face. I rotated my arm to experiment and the hand rotated too, but it didn't feel attached to me. I couldn't feel it moving where I was moving, and it freaked me out quite a bit.

I'm grateful Mother noticed me moving, jumped up, and came rushing over to the bed. She was very excited that I was awake. I tried to communicate to her I was conscious but having a hard time opening my eyes. My words weren't coming out right either. I told her something was wrong with my hand. Was that my hand? I wasn't sure it could be mine. It had to be Mom's, and I had to make her prove it to me as I lay there unable to move around yet. For the most part I could make nothing more than slight grunting sounds that tried to resemble words. Somehow, she figured out what I was trying to say.

Mother explained to me they had to pump me full of saline solution so they didn't have to use as much blood. They almost ran out of it as it was, but they had exactly the right amount to the last drop. She said because of the saline, I had twice as much fluid in my body as normal, and that was why everything was so puffy. The puffiness would go down, but that was why my eyelids were so hard to open too.

The doctors had become concerned that I may've ended up in a coma and weren't sure I was going to wake up at all. It had been three hours since they pulled me out of surgery. The surgery had taken three hours instead of an hour and a half due to undisclosed complications. It was also double the expected time for me to wake up from the anesthesia. They would not go into what had happened no matter how much I tried to talk them into it. With something like that, I can't help but wonder if I died. I thought that would have made a cool story to tell at that age.

Whatever happened, they were very relieved I was awake. They already had five Petri dishes stuck into my back to drain out excess fluids. They had to keep rolling me over and around. I became aware of my body as the last of the anesthesia wore off and began to realize I was in the most pain of my entire life. The doctor had told me that after this, having a baby would seem like a breeze. He wasn't kidding. I hurt so much I couldn't even breathe.

I tried to lay there as long as I could. I'd take the tiniest breath possible in or out, and then hold it until I absolutely had to take the next breath. I counted each millisecond out and it seemed to last an eternity. They had me on a morphine drip for the pain that I could push every seven minutes for another dose if I wanted. It hurt so much I kept pushing it for distraction. It wouldn't release anything for another seven minutes, but I didn't care. I must have been immune to the morphine - or allergic - because I don't think it did a thing for me to relieve the pain at all. I could feel it burn as it went into the vein from the needle for about a millimeter, and then it wouldn't do anything at all. I asked them to raise the dosage or, better yet, to use something different. It wasn't working but they wouldn't change it until I was able to start taking actual pain pills in a few days. I thought I would never make it that long until then.

I may have dozed off every once in a while for a minute or two during that first day as I lay frozen in pain. It was a little bit comforting in the back of my mind to know I was not alone. Mom was sitting there watching over me in these strange surroundings. Knowing she was there if I needed anything told me she cared. I hurt too much for her to hold my hand or even sit next to the hospital bed. So she sat in the chair where she had been when I had woken up after the surgery was over.

Once dinnertime and visiting hours were over, my mom told me she was going to leave for the evening to get some sleep. I was so afraid to have her leave me there all alone; I didn't know if I could handle the pain by myself. I tried to convince her to stay with me there and sleep in a chair or something, but she told me I would be all right. Nurses would check in on me all evening until the next morning when she returned. I felt the panic rising up inside of me, but I was in so much pain I couldn't even move to reach out for her as she left the room.

Anyone who has ever stayed in a hospital for more than a day, well knows that, it is impossible to sleep in one. There is always a nurse poking you. They ask if you're sleeping, see if you need anything, check your vitals, and try to see if you've had a bowel movement yet. There are strange beeps and sounds, and the other patients are noisier at night than during the day. I felt more awake than I had all that day. My pain was as great as ever. The morphine drip wasn't doing anything for me at all, so I thought I would try the television. I checked every channel, and most of them were hospital channels that had nothing but ads for drugs.

There is not usually anything good on TV at night anyway, even if you *could* get a real station in a hospital. After several frustrating minutes of trying to figure out how the TV system worked, I knew it was not going to help pass time. Watching the catheter bag fill with saline solution and fluids wouldn't help either. It was the longest night of my life.

After the first day, they came and had to fit me for the final adjustments to my fiberglass brace. They had pre-measured me for it in the months before the surgery. I would have to wear it for quite a few months until my back healed enough, so it needed to fit well and be comfortable. I remember they brought in what looked like a giant round straw with hip indentations. I knew then it was going to be a bad day.

I was exhausted after not sleeping all night and dealing with the pain the morphine didn't touch. Even the movements of the blood pulsing through my body made me scream inside my mind. It would have hurt too much more to have actually let out a yell. The brace looked way too long; it would end up going halfway down my legs. That would make it impossible to sit unless they sawed off the bottom to make it shorter. I had no idea how they were going to get me inside of it, and even once they did, it was round. I was more like a flat rectangular shape and would be bouncing around in all that extra space. There would be no support at all for my back.

I felt later that day like my spine had been completely removed in a vicious manner. On top of that, I was unable to move myself in any way. I had completely lost any and all muscle tone I once had and was only slightly above being in a vegetative state. The only thing I could imagine the nurses doing was to shove me in one end of the hole and threading me through the brace.

I was in so much pain I begged them to reschedule to do the fitting another day, but they could not. I had to have it so I could get up and start getting into physical therapy right away to prevent blood clots. I told them it was going to be impossible because everything hurt so much. I had been to physical therapy with my best friend who had been in a car accident before I broke my back. I knew what physical therapy meant.

They had a sneaky trick up their sleeves with that brace, though, and they had their orders. They showed me that they had cut the brace along one side. They could pull the cut side open and then they could pick me up and set me in it. I saw they could not open it up very far; the cut was jagged and rough, and I knew this was going to be a bad day. I had Petri dishes coming out of my back, IV's in my arms, oxygen tubes up my nose, and a catheter still in from the surgery. The brace was the smallest size they had. It was made for someone with a much longer torso and bigger around than I was. Even bloated up twice my size from all the extra saline in my body it was still way too big.

They had about six male and female nurses in there all struggling together to try and keep the brace open. At the same time, they lifted my limp, pudding-like body into the brace. I tried, but I was completely unable to assist in any way. They decided I was making it harder for them when I tried to help so I stayed as limp as possible. The jagged fiberglass raked across my hypersensitive skin and fresh stitches. It caught at the threads and ripped out Petri dishes along the way. They were doing everything they could to be super careful, and, I still couldn't help sobbing as they finally shoved me into the brace, tubes, hoses, and all.

I begged them to leave me inside so they wouldn't have to move me again. I had already guessed that getting me out was going to be much more difficult than putting me in had been. They discussed they didn't know how they were going to get me back out and that this brace was not going to work. They couldn't grab ahold of me again with the brace past my shoulders and arms far above my head and down almost to my knees. I didn't know it was possible to hurt more than I already did.

After much difficulty on everyone's part, and more crying on mine, they finally got me back out. We came to the conclusion that this brace was definitely not going to work by any means. I recommended they lay the thing down next to a person first to see if it would fit before putting them inside. It was *very* painful. They agreed that was a very good idea. I didn't think I could try doing that again even if they somehow came up with a smaller brace. I was grateful they did not.

Since the fiberglass brace was not going to work, they had to figure out something else. The doctor and the physical therapist said I absolutely *had* to have something. My back needed help supporting my body until my muscles were strong again. I felt like a limp rag doll flopping around. I knew they were right about having something to hold my back together while it healed. The doctor said I would need it or I would never be able to get up again.

I spent the rest of that agonizing day pressing my morphine drip button. I also alternated between watching Mom read a book or magazine and telling me things. I couldn't move much or make a sound due to the pain I felt every time I tried. The conversation was pretty one-sided as I listened to her talk about her visit with our cousins. I passed out every once in a while. Every second lasted an eternity as I tried not to breathe and keep from screaming. They told me most of the pain was coming from where they had removed some bone to fuse everything together.

I remember the hot tears would roll out of the corners of my eyes and back into my hair as I laid there. I was unable to even wipe them away. I could feel the salt building up as they kept running and running. Why wouldn't they give me something else that would numb the pain?

Pretty soon a woman came into my room and asked me if I was ready to go. I had no idea what she was talking about. She seemed surprised they hadn't told us they scheduled me to come to physical therapy that day. It was supposed to be right after I had gotten my brace. I tried to tell her I couldn't even move myself. I explained they hadn't been successful with the brace so I had nothing to support my back. She was not going to listen to anything I had to say.

She and a large hulking man brought in a gurney. They picked me up by the sheets and plopped me over, insensitive to the fact that I'd had back surgery. They were unsympathetic to my excruciating pain and began to strap me down in several places. I still had Petri dishes in my back and also hooked up to three IVs. They prepared to haul my morphine bag and fluids stand along. It was almost like they knew they were doing something they shouldn't. I sent my mom a look that cried for help as I tried to protest again. She went running to find the doctor to make sure they should even be taking me from the room like that without a brace.

I was in so much pain I couldn't handle the overhead lights going by as they wheeled me down the hallway. Excruciating pain was shooting through my body every crack in the tile they went over. They put something over my eyes as they kept going, but they were not happy. They both seemed so angry. Mom found a nurse and they began scrambling to find the doctor. They needed to make sure they were supposed to take me down there to physical therapy or not. The events earlier seemed to tell us that things should be postponed a little while to let me recover. We also were waiting to find out what they were doing for a brace. I felt like I got kidnapped in the hospital.

Once we reached the physical therapy room, they plopped me roughly onto another table. Then they strapped me in nice and tight everywhere and said that I wouldn't have to do anything but lay there. They moved fast. They said they had to get my blood circulating or I would develop blood clots and that could kill me. It might hurt, they said. It would feel like prickling needles all over my body as the circulation started moving.

The table onto which they had strapped me would tilt up at the head then tip the other way so that my feet were in the air. Then it would repeat the process over and over. I couldn't handle the steep angle and the pressure around the fusion and stitches pulling. They were very angry at me but backed it off and leveled it a lot so that it hardly tipped. It was still excruciating. I now knew what Hans Solo must have felt when they froze him in carbonite as everything began to explode around him.

The table was covered in vinyl and I was in an all-cotton gown and cotton hospital sheets. I was sure that I was going to slide off that table and splat into a gooey mess of liquid bones and a puddle of meat on the floor. Like Humpty Dumpty, I felt I would never be put back together again.

The table continued tipping one way then the other. Every bone in my back screamed from the pressure and the movement as gravity worked. It tried to move my blood like a giant roller coaster stuck in molasses. I felt as though they were pummeling me with mallets, had kidnapped me, and put me into a torture chamber of horrors. I tried to get her to stop so that we could try something different that didn't hurt my back so much. She told me I had to suck it up and get through this and that she wasn't going to let me get blood clots while she was around.

I did not appreciate her very much that day, to say the least. When she had finished with me, she told me I had done well but I would have to do much better the next time. She promised, much to my horror, that she would see me again the next day. That did *not* make me happy. My mother and I talked to the doctor about it after they had returned me to my room. He hadn't been too pleased that they had taken me without having my brace on. It could have created permanent damage, he said. I could hear him later talking outside my room with the physical therapist. They argued about what had happened. The therapist promised they would not take me again until I had a brace, but they better get me one before the next day.

The new brace that they had decided on for me was elastic and cotton with Velcro straps. It had rods that were sewn into the brace itself halfway from the middle of both sides of my spine. It looked like a corset with a second Velcro strap that reinforced around the waist. Once it was on, I would have two layers going around my torso holding everything together. It came down over my hips but would not interfere with my sitting down. Then it came right under my chest so that my rib cage was also inside.

I would wear the brace during the day, but not when showering and not at night while I slept. The muscles would need a break. After a certain amount of time, I would begin decreasing how long I wore it during the day until I no longer needed it. They showed me how to use it and how to put it on while I was lying down. Then I had to roll onto my side before pushing myself up into an upright position. They had to help me a lot as the surgery and lack of sleep had weakened me. They were very encouraging and confident I would be able to do these things on my own soon enough.

The first night alone without my mom there was terrifying. I felt so helpless and vulnerable. I needed some help with something very personal. I wanted a nurse to check if my menstrual cycle had decided to make an unexpected double house call that month. I was unable to even move myself at all.

I pushed the button asking someone to come by and in the door walked a male nurse. Most of the lights were out in the rooms and so there were only a few lights on in the hallway where the nurse station was. I was terrified! Being so young, I definitely was not comfortable talking to a male about what I needed help with. He could tell I was very uncomfortable. Being a first-time hospital patient, I had not even considered the idea that there was such a thing as male nurses.

The nurse finally got me to explain what I suspected might be happening to my body. I asked him if he could please send in a lady nurse to assist me. I didn't mean any offense to him; it was just a very personal thing. It horrified me my body had potentially betrayed me like this while I was in the hospital. I had been sure I wouldn't have to deal with this when I had come in for surgery.

The male nurse explained that there was only one lady nurse on the floor that night. She was getting lots of calls to help people with things. He said he understood and gave me the option to wait for her, which I took right away. A long time went by - it could have been an hour - and she still hadn't come.

I grew more worried about my predicament and not being able to do anything about it. I finally called again for the nurse and the same male nurse came by. I told him I couldn't wait any longer for the other nurse to come, so I would let him help me. He explained that it is very normal for women to have an extra period under a lot of stress. They were very used to helping people in the hospital with that quite often.

He was professional and very careful to get me situated. He didn't compromise my modesty or make me feel the least bit uncomfortable, for which I was very grateful. After another night of this going on, though, I didn't care anymore about anything. On top of what I was already going through, I was in so much pain, and everyone had to help me so much. I knew when the time would come to have a baby someday, I wouldn't be embarrassed at all. I wouldn't worry about having a doctor pulling a human being out of the most secret parts of my body. I completely lost all self-consciousness about myself after that experience. And I was right; when the time came for me to have children, I wasn't embarrassed at all.

I remember the first time I started feeling the bed sores from lying there so much that first and second day. The nurses were very good about coming, shifting me, and propping me with lots of pillows. They'd come every couple of hours before I got my back brace. My body was at the point where I could not handle reclining any longer with my muscles so thin now. There was no padding left and the very bones threatened to push right out through my skin. I begged Mom to come and help me to sit up. She hadn't thought that would be such a good idea. I insisted so much she had some nurses come in to help so we could make sure I wouldn't hurt myself.

They got on both sides of me and helped me into an upright position with great caution. They kept me lifted a little to avoid gravity's pressure on all the fresh wounds inside and out. They held my arms so that there wouldn't be so much weight on my spine either. It was so excruciating that I could not handle even a second of it. I begged them to put me back down again as fast as they could. I resolved not to do that again anytime soon. Bed sores were much preferred over the pain of trying to support any kind of weight on my back at that point.

One of the things that I thought about as I lay there was something that had happened to a family friend. He had been out somewhere working when a great big lightning storm rolled in. Thinking he would be fine since he didn't have much left to do, he finished up. He figured that afterward he would head inside to get out of the weather, but his timing and figuring were not in line with what happened next. A giant bolt of lightning hit the ground very near to him. It was so strong that it threw him across the grass where he lay as though he were dead.

Someone found him and rushed him to the hospital. They treated him there for very bad burns to his entire body, inside and out. They weren't sure if he would survive for quite some time. Anyone who has experience with lightning knows if you get hit, it blows out through your hands and feet. The worst of his burns were on his hands and feet.

As he shared his story one day during a visit, the symbolism of his hands and feet being burned the worst struck me. It was much like the Savior's wounds on the cross where he was nailed up. The symbolism was not lost on my friend either. He shared how he laid in the hospital and was in so much pain, more than he had ever imagined was possible to experience. He realized the Lord himself had experienced more pain than any one of us.

He talked about how Jesus took on all the pains and sorrow of each one of us, whether we accept his gift or not. My friend had a long time to think about it as he lay there day after day in the hospital. As he did, he began to appreciate more of what the Lord had sacrificed for us. He realized how much he must truly love every one of us to do such a miraculous and excruciating thing as that.

I now found myself in my hospital bed with non-functioning morphine. All I could think about was my Savior and, that he experienced this pain *I* felt and knew it in an intimate way as I did. I thought about how he had died for me on the cross. I thought of the excruciating pain and humiliation that led up to that event. How he resurrected the third day so that I could live again and be restored back to him.

I was filled with gratitude. I was filled with shame at my prideful nature. I was filled with wonder and amazement that someone could love me so much. He would go through so much pain to take on *my* sins. I felt my sins were so great I could not begin to repay him. They were beyond my ability to restore. It was not beyond his ability to cover my many shortcomings in his sight.

I wanted to take my own suffering from him so that he would not have to go through my part of it. I thought of all the horrible things that people do to each other and themselves on purpose. We don't realize the things we do to ourselves that are so damaging and painful than what I felt from this surgery. I knew he would pay and had paid for all these things for me already. I struggled to allow him to do this for me because I knew it was already a done deal. I was so willful and had struggled with my relationship with God so much. I didn't trust him - not in a real way. The days rolled on and on and my understanding of his love for me grew. I began to submit my heart to him.

They got the back brace in, put it on me, and had me ready in time to have another day at physical therapy. They strapped me down nice and tight to the table with a cloth over my eyes again for the bright lights. It was a little bit easier with the brace holding everything together. The Petri dishes had also been removed. Instead, there were giant bandages that had to be changed often.

The fear remained that I would slide off the table. The hot tears streamed everywhere; it was still extremely painful. It felt like ice picks stabbing every part of my body as the blood would try to move from one end of me to the other. This went on for minutes on end. The physical therapist at the hospital was merciless. Before my surgery I went to physical therapy with a friend for moral support. I had a newfound sympathy for what they might have been going through in their exercises. I wasn't prepared.

On the third day, they finally removed the morphine drip. They started allowing me to try taking pain killer tablets by mouth. I couldn't wait to try that instead, hoping that it would bring me even the smallest amount of relief. I had experienced none with the morphine. Within twenty minutes of taking the pain killers the pain began to subside some. It was enough that I was able to better bear the healing process. It was such a relief that it actually cut the pain down where the morphine had failed so miserably. I must have said a million prayers of gratitude that the pain killers worked. Now I only felt about half of the pain.

The most difficult thing about the pain killers were that I had to take them every four hours. They put me alone in charge of keeping track of when I was supposed to take them. I had no way to set a timer, no ability to move around by myself, and I usually fell asleep during the day. I tried to stay awake but I couldn't sleep at night, so I'd fall asleep. We had no timer, and I couldn't see the clock well. If I missed my next dosage by even ten or twenty minutes, I was back to ultimate pain for the next half hour to an hour. I had to wait until the pills worked their way into my system again. Despite my mother's and my best efforts, we missed my dosages quite a few times over the next days.

Several times every day I went to physical therapy to tip my blood around. Getting my circulation going again was preparation for what was coming. I had no idea what I was in for since this part had never been discussed with me prior to the surgery. Trying to sit up with the pressure and weight on my very sensitive low back and spine was enough to make me pass out. It took my breath away every time I had to go to therapy.

I was too weak in the hospital to pull the elastic Velcro straps across where they needed to be for the brace. I would work on it as time went by. The first time they had to have me lie on the bed and pull the straps around. They rolled me as they tried to navigate everything and keep my gown crossed over in the back. They got me set in the brace in my lovely hospital gown and now I no longer had to worry about it flapping open in the back. The brace did a very good job holding it crossed well over and in place. They completed my look with thick compression socks that went all the way up to my hips. I looked like I was inside-out high hospital fashion and wearing a girdle too. They whisked me straight down to physical therapy for what they had in store for me from day one. The exercise of the day: trying to stand and walk.

They had brought me to the physical therapy room in a wheel chair this time since I was now able to sit up. I'll tell you what, I still felt every single crack in those old stick down rubber tiles they have in the hospitals. I felt them all the way down and back as sure as if I was being pounded with a sledge hammer. They told me to stand up and hold onto the two support bars. I was going to be walking back and forth to help restrengthen the muscles and get my circulation going. I thought to myself, yeah right, I can't even handle sitting up here in this wheelchair with this back brace on. You want me to do all *that*?

I made my best attempt at standing up and wasn't able to on my own. This made the physical therapist really upset again. Too much time had passed after the surgery for me to be starting on this activity. This might permanently affect my ability to walk again, she said. I started to get scared, in large measure because I had never considered that I may not be able to walk again.

They got on both sides of me and tried to help balance and support me as I struggled to try and get myself upright. The strangest thing happened, though: my legs did not do what they were supposed to do. I did what I always did to stand, but the muscles didn't work at all. I couldn't feel them doing a thing, no matter how the fierce therapists commanded and yelled at me to stand.

All I could think was if this was it; we had done all this for nothing, and I was going to be paralyzed anyway. They attempted to raise me a couple more times, though I told them that my muscles were not firing. I was in so much pain that the confusion of what was happening didn't hit me until after I got back to my room later.

It was such a relief to be back at my room laying down again and getting all that hot burning pressure off of my back. They removed the brace, helping me with the greatest care onto my back and onto the pillows. I could hear the therapist talking with the surgeon and nurses about my predicament. They were right outside my room, and she argued about the problem with the brace not fitting the first day.

Her frustration mounted as she went on about so many days for the other one to get here. She was furious at my not being able to even stand by myself now. I felt the hot tears running with reckless abandon back along my cheeks. They trickled down into my hair, leaving thick salty trails as they continued. I was too tired to cry but in too much pain and emotional distress not to.

The surgeon was calm as he said things had not worked out the way that they had planned. There had been complications and they had to work with what they had from here on out. They all needed to do their best, and that was all they could do. His voice felt like soothing warm, melty butter to my mind. It wrapped my heart with a sense of security as I fell into unconsciousness, exhausted. My last thought gave him a *hurrah* for being so calm, patient, and confident that things would be okay.

One day and night ran into the next, and I couldn't even tell how long I had been in the hospital anymore. Mom ordered me all kinds of tasty things to eat that she thought I'd find exciting. She hoped they'd be even a little distracting from what was going on. It was a great comfort to have her with me during the day even though I slept most of it away except for physical therapy. I was always exhausted afterwards. After a few more attempts, we finally got me to where I could stand up from the wheel chair. I shook and wobbled around like a new baby making its first attempts to learn to stand.

The physical therapist was jubilant that I had finally gotten to stand, but she was still so fierce. She pushed me to walk now like her very career hinged on getting me moving. My leg felt like it was full of lead. I tried my very best to get it to move forward that first step but it jiggled and wobbled along with the rest of me. I had even used my arms to lean my body weight onto my other leg. My brain told my leg to move, to lift the knee, to take that step. It was like the signal was not getting there at all. It was the weirdest feeling in the world not to have my body obey my brain. I tried over and over as the therapist lashed me with her words that I could do it, take a step, come on!

I finally resorted to trying to lean even farther to the opposite side. I then used my body to sort of fling my leg around a little into a forward direction. It moved about an inch. I had a vice grip on those parallel bars as the therapist tried to help coax another bit of distance out of my legs. I could only fling my legs forward a couple of times before I was too exhausted to even stand. I was sweating as if I'd run a marathon. They had to help me back into the wheelchair and send me back to my room. I fell into an exhausted painful sleep until my next appointment where it happened all over again.

You never go through life thinking, "Someday I may have to learn how to walk again." You kind of take it for granted that once you learn to walk, you always will until you get too old and die. My brain had to reroute signals to my muscles to work. There had been 20% damage to the nerves during the surgery, and they told me that was very nominal. They had been very pleased to only have that much damage to the nerves in such a complex and delicate area of the body. There had been a lot going on in there they had to deal with. They were excited I was making such rapid progress, considering all the rerouting. Even the physical therapist could see that after a while and had to admit that I was trying as hard as I could to do the work.

Every day I had a death grip on those bars as my brain screamed at my body to move. I was able to fling-walk a few steps farther every time I went to therapy. I never felt like I had worked so hard and seen such little progress. I began to think that this would be the best it got. In time I would get strong enough arms and be fling-walking with one of those walkers for the rest of my life. It was not a pretty sight to conjure up in my mind. The fear helped me push my physical body as if my very life depended on me being able to walk again.

No matter how painful these exercises were for every move, I pushed myself to walk or die. In a way, my life *did* depend on it. I could not accept that I would not be able to walk again. I funneled the fear, frustration, and anger at that possibility into pushing myself. I mentally lashed myself with a whip to continue fighting for every inch of ground, no matter how I got it. Every time, I returned to my room to fall into an exhausted sleep. I often missed my pain medication, waking to bones screaming from physical therapy.

As it got closer to the end of my five-day stay at the hospital, they brought in a walker. It was the kind with the little wheels on the front and the stoppers on the back legs and the little handles on the top. Part of my next physical therapy appointment was to use the walker. I couldn't lift up the back end with the stoppers to allow the wheels to move forward. I couldn't even use my weight to push it forward because the back stopper legs kept tumbling back to the ground. They hit lopsided and hindered my attempted forward progression. I couldn't move so much as an inch.

I told them the walker wasn't going to work because I was not strong enough to lift it. It wasn't going to be functional for me. I don't know how in the world those little bitty old folks even can push those things around and go all over the place. To this day it still amazes me that they can do it. (My hat is off to you. You are amazing!)

We decided if I needed to do something, like to go to the bathroom or to the table, that my mother or someone would help me. I would hold onto her arm to get from one place to the other, and that's what we ended up doing. I had no idea I held onto her arm so tight in those days after we went back home.

A day or two later all these little finger and hand bruises started showing up all over her arm. They were from where I was hanging onto her for dear life when I had to walk. I felt so bad about that, but she never complained about it hurting or being sore at all. She smiled and said it was okay, it didn't bother her at all. Her arm looked like alternating stages of healing and new bruises for the next few months.

For most people, being in the hospital is not at all like they show it on television and the movies. There are not tons of flowers, balloons, and cards filling the rooms. The patients don't lay there all lovely and fresh looking, and it's not like a big family reunion. It's painful, lonely, and uncomfortable. You can hear sick people coughing and throwing up all night or calling for a nurse. The beds are hard, and someone is always waking you up to check your temperature or poke you with sharp needles. Most rooms don't have *any* flowers or cards or even visitors. Most people don't even have someone sitting with them during the day.

It was awful when they had to take out the catheter. It almost seemed to burn or like something got scratched when they put it in for the surgery. I had to start using the toilet once I was able to sit up again. It was uncomfortable coming out, and I could only imagine the same putting it in there in the first place. Mom would usually help me get to the bathroom and back during the day and I would have the nurses' help at night. They tried to get me back to doing things myself again before I left and before my organs completely forgot how to function.

By the time the end of the week rolled around and I could go home, I was so grateful for everyone's help. I didn't know if I would ever be able to walk, but I was sad to say goodbye to everyone, even the physical therapist. They wheeled me out to the car after I had changed into some very easy-to-put-on, soft, comfortable clothes. I was extra careful not to put any pressure on my back. We collected all our things in the big, stylish plastic hospital bags they gave us. Every crack in the flooring was still shockingly painful.

My goal was to be off the pain meds completely by the time my first bottle ran out. I vowed to not order a second bottle no matter how much it hurt. I took fewer capsules each day even though it was painful not to take more. It became a contest to see how little medication I could get by on. I wanted to get used to dealing with the pain when I wouldn't be taking them anymore. (It worked out fine and my body recovered much faster because of it, like the doctor had told me it would.)

We stopped and grabbed some burgers on the drive home before we left town. I discovered too soon that I would not be able to eat anything the whole way. A road construction company had attempted a temporary fix to the highway. It was in such poor condition and had many deep and wide cracks everywhere on the road. They sealed the cracks with tar, but the coarse pavement was extra bumpy, not smooth. I could feel every crevice of the road as if it had been magnified a million times throughout my entire body. Every single dimple and line washed over me like high-speed waves of biting, unrelenting pain.

At first, I told Mother to drive slower so I could try to deal with it for the next three hours straight. I knew the trip would now be even longer. She slowed down a lot and the bouncing of the vehicle increased so that I felt everything even more than before. Realizing it would take us longer to get back home *and* it was worse going slower, I begged her to drive as fast as she could. I hoped we would fly over some of the bumps in the road.

My poor mother didn't know what to do. She held back from crying. It was too much seeing me sobbing from pain and clinging to the back seat. I tried to stabilize myself the best I could as she raced for home. She told me stories so that I could focus on something else in second-long spurts to break up the pain. Even with the medication, it was the longest drive of my life.

When we finally arrived at home, Mom pulled the car as close up to the door as possible on the grass. I'm sure she must have felt exhausted too by the time we made it there, hearing me crying the whole way. My dad came out to help carry me inside. They brought my bed out into the living room close to the window that looked out into the front yard. I wanted to feel like a part of the family instead of being stuck in a bedroom all the time.

Mom gave me something so I could signal to her in the middle of the night if I needed to be rolled over or anything else. I would need her help so much over the next several months. The pain lasted a long time. It would be six months before I could walk in the most precarious manner on my own for short distances.

The back brace was my new best friend during the day. It was essential I wear it to support my back while strengthening and healing, but for protection too. Everything was always covered with a gauze bandage over the large surgical area. I was not allowed to even get my back wet for the first couple of months. First, I was only allowed sponge baths. Then I could tape plastic over the area for short, lukewarm showers to keep it dry, clean, and the tape from coming off. Though I would have preferred a warmer shower, my wound could not tolerate the heat. That was like heaven once I was able to finally take a warm shower again and enjoy it!

The surgeon had to cut my back open for the surgery. He had some great recommendations for us so that it would heal back up even and straight. If we followed his instructions, it wouldn't be that lumpy of a scar, either. One of the things he said was to rub aloe vera and vitamin E gel capsules around the stitches several times a day. Since I could not reach it by myself and I was not allowed to twist at all yet, my mother would do that for me. After it started healing up more, she sometimes had one of my other siblings take a turn. They were usually too grossed out by it to do it much.

After a while, everyone got tired of me being such an inconvenience. My bed took up the whole living room, and my back needed *gross* stuff put on it several times a day. I needed help with everything all the time. People don't mind helping babies because they are cute and little. It is difficult for a family to deal with a person old enough to take care of themselves who requires long-term care. God bless those caregivers who stick to it and are there for you when you need them! They are true angels.

The family usually sat at the table for dinner. They brought a plate in for me to eat until I could attempt to sit at the table with them. Sometimes they came in and joined me eating in the living room, and that was nice. We had never done that before, hardly ever, so it seemed like we were being naughty. Still, it didn't last too long after some of the kids kept spilling drinks and food too much.

The first time I attempted to sit at the table was a very memorable experience for me. We had wooden chairs with carved backs. I was very cautious as I sat down because I still had some nerve damage and had to be very careful. My body overreacted to any sense of touch to the areas involved. I miscalculated where my body was and slid back too far in the seat. Part of the carved back rest stuck out, and I found it. The chairs had all these fancy curves and shapes sticking out everywhere. I used to think they were beautiful, but from that moment on, they were more like medieval daggers, weapons of war. The second my back touched it I was greeted with a hot, searing sensation of obliterating pain. It removed any sense of healing and improvement that I thought I had made. After that, I always made sure to sit at the very front of the seat to be sure nothing would touch my back.

I made the mistake of thinking it would be comfortable to lean back and rely on the support of the chair and relax. The same thing happened when I was finally able to go to church for the first time. I thought the cushioned seats would be soft enough to lean against. I got the same hot searing pain as when I sat at the dining room table. I would have to sit forward in all my chairs until my back had healed up enough to do anything else. Luckily for me, my back brace had metal rod supports. It also had crisscrossing Velcro straps that held me up almost as if I *could* lean back in a chair.

A few of my friends would come by to see me from time to time. They told me what everyone was up to and would see how I was doing. After a while, though, we ran out of things to talk about. When you have nothing interesting going on in your life, you stop being interesting. The big events of *my* life were changing bandages and trying to walk an extra step that day. I couldn't expect people to put their whole lives on hold for me while mine was. Their lives were still moving forward and the gap of dissimilarity between us grew. After a while, the visits got farther and farther apart.

I realized how lonely my situation was as the weeks dragged by. I realized how broken and desolate I felt. I started to think no one - no man, for sure - would want a gal who was broken, especially as broken as I then was. No one was going to find me, trapped in my parent's home like that, for the rest of forever.

Like hungry wolves, desperation and loneliness took turns feeding off of my soul. I felt myself spiraling downward into the dark pit of despair. I started not to care about my life anymore. I had spurts of desperation and trying to push myself harder because I did not want to stay the way I was. It seemed like eternity dragged on with little progress.

One day ran into the next. I'd get up, have some version of a shower, apply oils to my scar, and bandage the surgical area up. The tenderness finally began to fade, but as it did, it seemed my hope for a normal life faded further too. Week by week went by until I finally became mobile enough to roll myself over in bed at night. I didn't have to only sleep on my side or stomach anymore, and they were able to move my bed back into my bedroom. The scenery had changed, but not much else.

I felt horrible every time Mom had to come out in the middle of the night and turn me to prevent bed sores. She worked so hard already taking care of Dad and all the rest of our family and all their various activities. Everyone in the whole household was so relieved the day my bed was finally able to be moved back into my room.

My siblings all made it very clear how much of an inconvenience I had been to them. I had embarrassed them because they didn't want to bring their friends over to the house all summer. They went on about how my back smelled weird and stunk up the house with the antiseptic that I had to keep on it. It made me feel even more unloved and unwanted, and I had been struggling with those feelings already. It didn't seem to matter to them that I had no control over those things. They wouldn't accept my apologies about the situation or how bad I felt about it.

When I was finally able to hold myself more upright, I started to feel like I was much stronger than I actually was. I was sure it was time to stretch my legs a bit, so I told my mother I wanted to go for a walk around the block. She was pretty sure I was not ready for that. I felt like I *was* strong enough, so I convinced her to go around the block with me towards the house of someone we knew. If I needed to take a break, we could there. The worst-case scenario was if I couldn't make it, she could leave me by the sidewalk, go get Dad and the car, and drive me home.

Mother went along with my plan for a walk around the block with quite a bit of resignation. As we made our way down the sidewalk with great, hesitating steps, I felt so jubilant in the morning air. I was sure I would make it all the way around and back to our house. We made our painstaking way onto the street, with me gripping my mother's arm as she supported me. Every once in a while, we stopped and rested a second, and she asked me if I wanted to turn back. I still felt strong, so I wanted to continue. I could see her glancing back towards the house. I'm pretty sure she didn't think we were going to make it to the end of the street, and she was right.

The neighbor saw us coming along the road as she glanced out of her window that morning. She headed down to her front door, called out to us, and asked us in to sit for a spell, knowing about my condition. She visited with my mother while I took the glass of water she handed me and tried to catch my breath. She was a personal trainer and checked my pulse to make sure I was okay once I had sat down. They were very kind about the whole thing and chatted about unimportant things. It was soothing to me. She called our house to let my dad know he needed to bring the car down to collect me.

I was so exhausted, my entire body shook from the effort of all that strenuous walking. As my dad came and scooped me into the car, I decided I was not going to be trying that again anytime soon. Every Sunday we went to church, I got to practice walking very short distances. I practiced around the house until I could get from one chair to another without a death grip on my mom's arm. Finally, I could get around without her help for little spurts until I was able to walk on my own. I began to learn that I had to take things slower for my body than was good for other people. It was better for me to take my time, but it took me many more trials in my life to realize this life lesson.

I remember one late summer day I had gotten to the point that I could get around a little on my own if I was very, very careful. A big group of my friends got together from all over town to play kick-ball or softball or something. I went and watched them from up on the bleachers. I longed to be out there playing, to be running with the others and having fun. The sun went down as I watched them play, and it was a beautiful sunset that night. It was a bittersweet experience. There was first the jubilation of showing up to one of the events. Then there was seeing everyone and the sadness of non-inclusion.

A couple of friends said "hello" and "good to see you" as they were leaving to walk out to their cars after the game ended. The sky was a brilliant orange, fading into the darker night sky. The air was perfect. It was pleasantly cool as the sun went down. I had a sense that, like the day was ending, so too was my life as I had known and expected it to be.

As I became more mobile, I started to develop a sense of fear about my future. I would be unable to lift anything heavy or sit or stand for long periods of time. There were so many restrictions placed upon how I would live my life with metal in my back on a permanent basis. I asked my previous employer if they could use any help around the office, but they already hired someone. There wasn't *quite* enough work for me to come back too. I was so afraid I wouldn't be able to do anything for work now. I had hoped they would feel sorry for me and let me come back to work for them until I figured things out. I didn't know what I would do, but they told me I should try back in a couple of months because the person they hired might leave soon. They would be happy to have me back as soon as I was ready and strong enough.

I had a goal to work toward and a greater sense of purpose and drive: to get stronger and become even more mobile. When I was finally able to try to go back to work, I was only able to stay for about thirty minutes to an hour. By then I was exhausted. I had to take my time and be patient while I tried to build up to being able to work part time hours over the next few months. It was so frustrating that my body couldn't do everything it used to do that I had taken for granted. I didn't think I had taken them *so much* for granted. I saw people walk and do things without a thought. I was filled with great wonder at how they didn't even think about it.

My grandpa always talked about gratitude. It was from his example that I began to practice more what he had been teaching me my whole childhood. He always talked about appreciating your eyes and the beauty of God's wonders that he created that you can see. He talked about your ears and the beautiful sounds you can hear. He talked sometimes about how amazing our hands are and the things that they can do. He also talked about the people you can help, and the things that you can make.

The best part of this experience was I got out of doing dishes, making my bed, and cleaning the shower for many years. I got to stay home in bed watching television all day long for quite a few months. Still, any enjoyment I could have gotten out of that was tarnished by the pain of healing and my loneliness. I was overwhelmed with the frustration of not being able to do anything. I felt abandoned and lost. I had a lot of time to think about the many people who are lonely, in pain, and suffering in this world. I thought about our responsibility to each other even more than I had been aware before the surgery.

My service-oriented parents allowed me to experience helping our neighborhood and town. God taught me another line, another principle of what I had learned so far. I know there is no way I could have made it through this trial as well as I did without my little bit of faith in God. I couldn't do it without faith that he is there and that he has all power to perform miracles. But, he often makes us work for them. We don't always recognize his hand in everything that we do. Sometimes it is years, or decades later – or more - before we have the wisdom and experience to see what he has done for us. If we are patient, watchful, and stay faithful, we will see.

After a lot of very hard work and struggle, I finally made it back to working again - even full time. I met someone and was able to move forward with my life. I can say my life experiences up to this point prepared me for the rest of my life. I can see that this is a time in which my own quest for healing began. After I was faced with death, it made me question my existence and mortality. I began to take stock of my life and what things are most important.

Chapter 3
Deep Sleep

I'M SITTING HERE WRITING, not knowing what to write about. I find it ironic to write my story for a book titled "Member Heal Thyself." My health condition has left me in a completely vulnerable and helpless state. It seems I am exhausted after even the smallest of efforts. My husband, for example, has to do all the household chores almost all the time.

I've had days on end where I've been so exhausted that I could feel myself becoming part of the couch upholstery fibers. I was too weak to get up out of bed by myself without the help of my Relief Society sisters coming and rolling me over. They would have to raise me up, make me breakfast (and sometimes feed me!), and help me to the shower. I tried to work on days that I had any strength. I had to work at temporary desk jobs for a day or at most a week. Any time I could work, I ended up paying the metaphorical pied piper for an equal amount of time.

Well-meaning friends, past boyfriends, family members, and even doctors tried to diagnose me. They guessed I had everything from depression, bi-polar disorder, diabetes, anxiety, and PTSD (post-traumatic stress disorder). They also tried to suggest I had anorexia or bulimia and a whole bunch of other things I didn't have. None of the tests came back as being positive, but they still tried to prescribe me drugs for things I didn't have. I could tell it frustrated them all I wouldn't just take drugs I didn't need simply because they tried to give them to me.

I realized that they didn't have my best interests at heart. I finally found someone who said my adrenal glands were shot from too much stress. That made the most sense but I was still left feeling like there was more to it than that. I kept searching for answers to what we were missing as the process went along.

I learned people would rather jump to conclusions based on a single remote similarity to something they've heard of. They want to label you with something out of their own convenience and be done with you. They'd rather move on to someone else or some other topic. I'm not sure if they are not interested in helping or lack the knowledge to help, in addition to wanting to look smart. There seem to be few who have adequate ability, as the hands of Christ, to help a person towards their healing.

I have seen the hands of healing angels that peeled back layer after layer of wounds and dis-ease in my life. In turn, I have been able to be one of those angels on more than one occasion to other people.

What a great blessing to help a person find the wholeness and completeness we all search for! I've learned we can't help someone else without turning to God and get his help for ourselves first. This is the most important and must be the very first thing we do.

God knows everything, from the beginning to the end. He knows our hearts best of all. We cannot - do not - see as well as God does. I have felt on occasion his great love for different, specific individuals. I have felt his love for me too. I have felt this love for people in my family and people with whom I've been privileged to work.

If you don't yet know this about yourself, I wish I could begin to convey to you how precious and well-loved you are. What you feel about yourself or what others may have tried to teach you can be very false. The love God has for you is perfect and is in spite of what you have or have not done. His love for you is also in spite of what others have and have not done to and for you.

Compare this to something that you cherish: a child, a hobby, a mentor, a loved one. Think about the strongest you have ever felt love for that person, place, or thing. Know that God's love for you goes beyond that multiplied the world over, and then some more.

I had a great aunt who passed away some years ago. This aunt was a very special woman in my life and to all those who knew her. She had a very special gift that she shared with others and was quite unique to her. You may know someone with a similar trait. It is my belief that God has planted these angels all around the globe like beacons of light and hope.

She listened to me about my struggles and then she touched my face with so much love. She looked me in the eye and told me how much she loved me and I felt the truth of it. I felt God's love for me come pouring through too, and it would seem as though all space and time stopped. It was so powerful I wondered how I had ever forgotten being loved so much.

Have you ever seen the face of God?

It was in those moments with my great aunt that I felt his strong love for me. He was so close to me, on the other side of these eyes gazing upon me - it felt so strong. It was those moments, sacred and reverent, that filled me with the desire to try harder. I wanted to do and be better at all the many things I fell so short on, and still do.

At the same time I knew I was perfect the way I am, in his love. This knowledge allowed me to release Satan's greatest tools he uses still, guilt and shame. It gets us to hold ourselves back from moving forward into the happiness God has in store for us. That happiness is waiting for us all the time; all we have to do is step into it.

Many of us may feel like we don't see any sunshine down the road in front of us. We'd like to, but it doesn't seem to be anywhere. All we see is...nothing...or darkness...a wall with no end or a big, tall, foreboding mountain of the unknown. If you see the sunshine, great! Stay in the light! If you are among those of us who can't see the sun (or it keeps disappearing), then you should be excited.

Page 118

God sent his Son to heal our wounds, bind up our hearts, and help us find our greatest joy in this life - if we let him.

God sent his Son, Jesus Christ, to heal our wounds, bind up our hearts, and help us find our greatest joy in this life if we let him.

Jesus did not come in doom and gloom. He arrived with angels shouting hosannas and bringing good tidings of great joy. His purpose was to bring about the Father's will.

· In the book of Doctrine and Covenants (D&C) 136:29 it tells us to call on the Lord that our hearts may be joyful.

· In D&C 128:19 it says God is *joy*! His voice is one of gladness. As you come closer to him you can hear it – gladness, joy, mercy from heaven, truth in gladness and great joy! Beautiful are the feet of those who bring these messages and share them in joy and gladness.

· In D&C 101:36 it says that our joy is full in Him, where it cannot be full in this world where we live. The more we seek him and seek to live our lives by his example, the fuller our joy will be.

Man is that he may have joy, after all.

God knows some of us are pretty stubborn, strong-willed, and determined to do it on our own. We make the mistake of thinking our way is better, that we know more than he does. He loves us enough to let us find out his way *is* better, easier in the long run, and better for our growth and development. He knows sometimes we need convincing, even if we hurt ourselves or others in the process. He understands our imperfect experiences here on Earth color our perspectives on the truth.

He knows it looks different to each one of us and he tries to get us to clean our metaphorical lenses. We often don't even recognize truth for what it is anymore. We don't want to admit our hearts were hurt and we're afraid. We forget how to trust, which adds to our layers of dirty and colored lenses of life. We forget God; we forget we can trust him. We're so afraid of the painful experiences with the limited amount of knowledge we started this life out with.

Misperception's effect on how we see everything else in life can be compared to a pair of glasses. It has many layered lenses that have a pivot point on the outside corner. As we go through life and experience pain or joy, we add new lenses on top of the other lenses there. All the lenses are different. Some are clear but have a smudge or a spot, some are dusty, some pink or orange, some are covered in a greasy film of goo.

After a while, it can get to be difficult to see out of these glasses. We never realize the lenses are there in the first place and would need cleaning on a periodic basis. Misconceptions and misperceptions are the things we misunderstand in life. It can be words, thoughts, feelings, and experiences. As you get rid of these lenses - or clean them - you are then able to see more clearly what things *are*.

Life can be so full of disappointments. Some are so large and obvious they can't be ignored, and they are easily felt and recognized. They sit there like a big black pit, yawning open to consume any happiness that dares attempt to approach it. Other disappointments are so small, they're easily missed and go overlooked. These can lie in wait, hidden for years, sneaking into our lives in what seems like unassociated ways. When they do appear, they wreak havoc in our lives and show up as various forms of loss. Some are so big we cannot deal with them, so we try to ignore or bury them deep inside, hoping they will go away. They don't.

If we are not extremely watchful and prayerful, we continue on unaware of the causes of our trouble. With God's help - and our efforts to heal - we may become aware of what the real cause of our pain and disappointment is. God does not want us to hold onto these things. When he commands us to lift the burdens of others, he doesn't mean to pick up someone's baggage and add it to ours. He wants us to help each other where and when (crucial to remember) it is needed and wanted. We should not be picky about where or how we serve God. When we are slow to answer God's call, he remembers and is also slow to answer our own calls. Choose to serve when and how he asks and you too will be blessed beyond measure.

Chapter 4
The Work

EVERYONE HAS SOMETHING going on in their life. In my experience, everyone has experienced at least one traumatic event. Many have experienced a lot of them. What one person may consider no big deal, another may find that same exact situation unbearable, and vice versa. It may even render them nonfunctional. Some people are very good at covering up their struggles. They may appear to have the perfect life and everything you could ever hope to be and have. Quite often you will find that they still have their own burdens to bear, much like you. The difference in how they look sometimes is what they decide to do about it.

It can feel like our situation is completely hopeless. It may seem like there is nothing that we can do to help ourselves. Sometimes, this may be true for a time while things are outside of our control. Sometimes, we actually need someone to intervene. We need someone to help get us started in the right direction. Sometimes, we need someone to help us remove the thing that has us pinned down so that we cannot move or breathe.

There is always hope. God is there for us, and we should always call on him first. He will be there with us on our journey, but he expects us to do the work. He lets us have the blessings of experience and the rewards of overcoming our own trials. He believes in our abilities and knows that we are stronger than we think.

This chapter is about our part; it is about doing the work. Pray like everything depends on God, and then work as if everything depends on us. Like a butterfly emerging from its cocoon or a chic from its egg, if we are to thrive and live, we must emerge on our own.

Scientists have found if you open the cocoon of a butterfly, it takes away the struggle of fighting its way out. The butterfly dies shortly after the cocoon has been opened. The same happens with baby chickens when they are starting to hatch. Break them free from their shell so they don't go through the process of fighting their way out, and they also die. The realization scientists made about the need to break free is very important. It is also very important to us and our development as much as it is for butterflies and chickens.

We do not break free from cocoons, and we do not breaking out of eggshells. *We* break free of falsehoods, wrong traditions, and bad ideas and habits. It takes everything we've got to break out of them. Things have been handed down by our ancestors, and we've gotten some others through our own weakness. When we let the wrong things go and honor all the right ones, we can experience life in a completely different way. The right things bless and honor those around us and ourselves.

We can choose to stay where we are. We can choose to make others feel more comfortable by joining them in not progressing. But that doesn't benefit anyone. Instead, we can honor the best within us and likewise those around us by choosing to heal. Choosing this will elevate those around us as we raise our own healing vibration. This happens as we strengthen and lift ourselves to new heights.

I have tried to write this book in a manner that is easy for many readers to read and understand. I hope its simplicity will encourage you to begin to put your own life in balance. Though the steps sound easy, you will find that the work will be some of the hardest you have ever done. You will not succeed on your first try, and you can't do it once and be done. You will feel like giving up at some point or another. It will either be because it seems far too simple or because it feels much too difficult.

Realize when you feel either of these that you are hitting an incredible obstacle: the fear of change. Learn to recognize the wall for what it is. Keep pushing on a little longer and you will overcome it and be on the other side of that wall very soon. When you feel it loom over you, you are right at the very peak of the mountain of what needs to be released. It cannot hurt you anymore. If you can push through it a little bit longer, it will all dissolve away. You will realize you have accomplished something wonderful. You will feel a lightness you hadn't before noticed.

Each section in this chapter addresses some of the most important things each one of us needs and each section will build on the next. I recommend that you try to do each one in order as each section helps the next one go a little bit easier. Do not underestimate the importance of each section. You may need someone who is an expert in that field to help you to succeed. Make sure to seek out professional help when dealing with a difficult section. It will be well worth your invested time and money. Look for the best expert you can. The most expensive choice is not always a sign of expertise and experience, but sometimes it is. Do your research.

SECTION 1
HYDRATION

HYDRATION is a very important topic when we talk about the physical work that must be done. Our bodies are mostly water. We must maintain our water reserves so things can work the way they need to work. Our bodies can't clean out the garbage inside of us if we're all dried out! We can't sweat to keep our body temperature even. Nutrients have a hard time getting to every cell without a river of transportation to get there. Hindering these processes can also cause and contribute to other health problems down the line.

In therapeutic massage sessions, this is one of the topics that I cover with clients. I try to find out how much water they are currently drinking when they first come in to see me. This can make a big difference in how much benefit they will receive from the work we will do that week. The muscles have a much more difficult time relaxing if they do not have enough fluids in them. They can't flush out the toxins released during the massage if they're dehydrated.

People often come in looking to get a massage to be able to feel more relaxed. They experience a lot of stress in their life every day, and it builds up. The body accumulates lots of lactic acid and other things that we refer in the massage industry as toxins (different than chemical toxins). They make you feel stiff, crunchy, and less flexible. Inflammation can be mistaken for being overweight and cause pain in the body. When people come into my office, my goal is to re-educate them about their bodies. I try to teach them how to use their body more effectively so that they can feel much better a lot more often. I like to think of it as finding the owner's manual for the body.

The owner's manual for the body is not like an owner's manual for a car. Bodies are not all the same with different exterior colors. We all have similar parts like a car: organs, limbs, and feelings. But that's where the similarities end. Every single body has different needs and requirements. We have different weaknesses and strengths. We have different levels of where we are in our body's condition and lifestyle. If you learn to listen to your body's signals about how things are running, you can prevent a lot of problems. It tries to talk to you about its needs and sends you little messages when it is struggling. There are little maps all over the body that show where problems are. Done the right way and with the right intent, massage helps to teach these things.

The body is very intelligent. It does not like substitutions and recognizes knock-offs. It can work with what it is given, but there is always a price. When you put it into a bad position, it is designed to survive at all costs - including costs to itself if need be. It will put you in jeopardy to get your attention and to try to save itself.

Our modern culture does not honor or respect the needs of the body. It's more like we live a life of slavery. Society teaches us to dishonor our needs at every turn. It tells us to work harder, faster, and cheaper until we die. It's all about the buck. While money is important and a wonderful tool, we must honor our body's needs and the needs of others. We need to remember that we are *not* a tool for money.

Many times, I have found that my new clients drink a lot of soda or pop or energy drinks or processed fruit juice and hardly any water throughout the day. These are liquids, but soda has many things in it that actually steal your nutrients and energy. Everything from the carbonation to the sugar is poisonous for you. The diet soda is even worse for the body than regular soda as the substitute sweeteners do a number on the body. Energy drinks are too high in things that actually poison the body as well in other ways. Both seem to cause a lot of inflammation in the body from what I have been able to see. Juice purchased from the store is not much different than soda because of the way it is processed. You're better off eating fresh fruit.

What the body wants is water - pure and clean water. It prefers no additives, preservatives, added fluoride or chlorine, and no toxic waste. The first thing that I like to address is the quantity of water a person is drinking of actual water daily. One client finally admitted to me she was only drinking a thimble sized amount of water a day, and felt like that was a lot. She did not prefer the taste of water at all, and I know many of my clients do not. Consider if you may have a water allergy, which needs to be diagnosed and addressed by a professional. I will discuss this more in the section Importance of Foods.

I had a client who came in complaining of feeling tired a lot. After a bit of discussion, she revealed she always drank soda at work. It was available in unlimited quantities, free for the employees and their guests. She never drank any water. She loved soda, especially caffeinated sodas. She felt it gave her that boost of energy when she started hitting a low point in the afternoons.

I suggested that she experiment: try to incorporate more water into her diet. The goal was to get her water intake up to the required amount her body needed. We would do this over the course of several weeks, I said, which would allow a slow change so the body could adjust. She agreed the week that followed her appointment, she would trade out one of her sodas for water. She would do this every day until her next appointment.

When she returned the next week, she reported that it had been very difficult for her to do. Basically, she hadn't done it at all. We went ahead with her appointment, and I focused on some areas that would help her to be able to move through some of these emotions. She agreed to try again the next week: she would make the first drink of the morning bottled water. The rest of the day, she would drink her sodas as usual, as many as she wanted. This even meant she still drank the same number of cans of soda as before the challenge to drink the water.

When my client returned the next week, she was so excited that she couldn't wait to tell me what had happened to her. She had drunk the water bottle first at the beginning of the day as planned. Then as the day went on, she found that she felt a little better. She didn't *want* the extra can of soda that she had replaced with water. She was so surprised that she felt so much better that she wanted to jump in and increase her water all at once. I advised that she take it slow so that she didn't put her body into shock. Now she had done a week of one water bottle a day, she should try two a day in place of her sodas. Then we would change out three or more depending on how many she felt that she needed and wanted.

Soon, she worked her way up to completely switching out her sodas for water bottles. Every time she switched out a can, she felt more and more energy. Her mind was clearer and she felt much happier - she seemed like she was going to burst every time I saw her. She grew so excited about her own results that she became an advocate for water at the office with her co-workers. She would run up to the guys getting a soda and trading them for water so they would feel better too. She was very likeable and vivacious, and so she had good results with her co-workers. Soon they reported similar results, and the owner traded the soda machine for a water cooler.

When the body gets dehydrated, it's like a shriveled raisin inside or the hard and dry, cracked desert floor. When the rain comes all at once what happens to the water? Anyone living in a desert can tell you: you wind up with a big flood. The water runs right off almost like it was concrete. Why? The ground is hard and cannot absorb the water even though water is exactly what it needs. The soil has not been prepared. The water runs right off of it, much like a raisin if you run it under the water.

The best way to get the ground ready is to prepare it. Have a nice little sprinkle at first a few times. Add a little bit more each time you water and then a little bit *more* water. This allows that tiny bit to seep into the upper layer of the dirt. If you don't wait too long, the dirt will still have the moisture in it.

The next sprinkle will allow that water to penetrate a little bit deeper and even deeper the next time it rains. The ground's ability to hold more water grows as it is given small increases of water. Over time, it is able to hold great amounts of water at once. The body is the same way. If you drink too much at once, it will flood out of you, flushing out all your minerals. It will drown brain cells. I don't know about you, but as I'm getting older, I could do with keeping the brain cells I have left alive and well.

My general recommendation for how much water you need to drink depends on a few factors. First, you should be getting half your body weight in ounces of actual straight *water* a day. To figure this out take your current weight - be honest; I know we all like to fudge here a little but don't cheat, trust me – then divide that number by 2. That's how many ounces per day recommended for you.

As your weight begins to change, that number for how much water you drink daily will also change. For example, if I weighed 200 pounds,

I would divide 200 by 2, which equals 100 ounces of water to drink. This is the amount for an average person who sits indoors all day and never does anything active. It is for someone who has no stress. It's for a person who does not take prescription medication or use recreational drugs. It is for a person who does not eat a diet high in acidic, processed foods.

200 lbs. ÷ 2 = 100 oz.

Once you have your ounces for the day, it's pretty easy to kind of ballpark how many bottles of water you will need to drink. You can choose to use bottled water or use a drinking container you like. Make sure it tells how much it holds. Some water bottles will hold eight ounces, twelve ounces, sixteen ounces, or even liters or gallons.

Remember: the amount of water you have to drink does not mean anything bad. I have a brother that is stick thin, thin as a rail, who has to drink two gallons a day. He is over six feet tall. Another of my relatives is in great shape and also has to drink two gallons a day. He is five feet tall but has body builder muscles and heavy, solid bones. Body mass is distributed in many ways.

If you take prescription medications, it is vital you consult with your physician about your extra water intake needs. Many prescription drugs need a lot of extra water for each drug that you are taking.

If you are not getting enough water, you may be damaging organs and body systems without even realizing it. If you are on a lot of medications, it may be a sign that it's doing a lot of damage already. You will need to drink a lot *more* water than half your body weight in ounces a day. Your doctor can help you figure out how much.

For those of you who take lots of medications and wish you could get off of them, there is some good news. Get your water balanced first. Then get the other areas of your life back in line, and you may be able to cut your medications down. I have seen most of my clients on medications cut them in half, then in half again. We always work with their doctors to help check the medication dosages. Many of them were able to get completely off of *all* their medications in the time I worked with them. The body is designed to heal itself under the right conditions. If you give it the tools and effort on your part, you can keep it in good working order. Your body will take care of you if you will take care of it.

Some of you may be ill or under stress, even huge amounts of stress; it is the world that we live in. If you fall into this category then you also need more than the average amount of water. Make sure to get professional help to determine the right amount of water to take. Always remember you should begin changing your water intake slowly. You don't want to flush out your nutrients and drown brain cells. It's always a good idea to swap out sodas, and energy drinks (and so on) for water first. Trade them out in equal quantities before adding more liquid to your diet than you're used to daily. You could get sick or hurt yourself if you aren't careful, and we don't want that to happen.

For those of you concerned that drinking lots of water will make you fat, you can rest assured this is not the case. You have to drink more water in accordance to your weight number. Some people think if it is high, it means they are fat. This isn't necessarily true. Let me show you some information that you can get behind.

Studies from wellness to medical journals show drinking water actually helps you *lose* weight. It helps boost your metabolism. It decreases your appetite. The body often signals dehydration in a way that feels like hunger. Drinking water in the right amount helps us to shed excess water weight. If you feel hungry, first get a drink of water. You might just be thirsty! Drinking water to lose water weight seems counter-intuitive, but if the body feels there's a drought, it's going to try to stock up on water like a cactus. You eventually want it to feel more like a rain forest in your body than the Sahara Desert.

Quite a few people wanted to lose weight as part of their massage therapy goals as well as other things. They lost up to thirty pounds in the first month. One client went on to win a gold medal in grappling. He lost weight, gained lean muscle, which made him stronger, and gave him an advantage over his fellow competitors. The only thing all my clients changed was the first step: the water they drank and how they drank it. They didn't add exercise or change their diet at all. For people who *do* change more of their lifestyle we can see wonderful progress.

Massage therapy teaches you how to live a life of balance. It teaches you to be in harmony with yourself and with those around you as well. But, people around you who are not in harmony with themselves will still be out of harmony. They will most likely be out of harmony with you too, until they get there. Be patient with yourself and with them. It's a long road. The point is that there is hope for us all if we want to become better and live richer, more fulfilling lives.

You don't know what you are missing until you experience it and realize how much you've been missing. The deeper you go, the more you realize there's another whole layer of discovery. That is when things start to get very exciting! If you choose to try out this first experiment I would love to hear from you about and how your experience is going. Water is an essential part of every living thing, and it carries life. Without it we are dead - physically, mentally, and spiritually.

SECTION 2 IMPORTANCE OF FOOD

AFTER WATER, the food we eat is the most essential to living that we know of. It is one of the greatest things about which we need to make good decisions if we desire to be disease free and well. The supermarkets are now filled with things that look like food but do little to fill you with nutrition. Hidden names of secret ingredients have replaced real ones. Produce is harvested before it is ready. Do your research. Avoid pesticides and genetically modified organisms (GMOs). They are not good for the body; I speak from personal experience. Be sure to make good choices and speak up to your grocery stores and say you want real food. Grow your own produce where you have space to do so. Put your health first, because ruthless companies' marketing priority is how to make as much money as they can. Many of them don't care how they get it.

We shop in a make-money-first, predatory, addiction-driven culture. It puts us in a frenzy to look for foods with more crunch factor. We crave foods that are fattier, saltier, spicier, sweeter, with ever brighter colors. When we eat foods that are fast, easy, and exciting, it leaves us burnt out, overstimulated, and starving. What is a person to do? We can take the attitude of "if you can't beat them, join them," but that's not good for the body. It is definitely an easy route to take, and we find many people on that path. The road is wide and smooth. With everything that we have going on and as tired as we get, it seems to be the only realistic option. Sometimes we don't even know there is another option. The climb is steep, the trail is narrow, and there are boulders to climb over, but the view is fantastic. When you get to the top you feel so strong! What other road is there? The road to real food is the one we cook and prepare ourselves and that nourishes us. It doesn't take any more time to do, it gives us more energy than the other option, and many times it is much more affordable too. Did I mention it tastes great too?

To take this different path you have to admit to yourself there is a pervasive problem in the food industry. There are tons of articles about this, books, studies, and findings. They talk about how pesticides and processed sugars affect the body. You only need look and want to find the information. I am not going to get into it, but you can research if it you like. I would even recommend doing so. This section is about the importance of foods. I want to point out there are people working against real food - *good* food - to make money. You have to take a very proactive approach to stand your ground on doing what's best for your body now and in the future.

God gave us wholesome herbs for our many different constitutions, natures, and uses. These are foods that strengthen us. They should be used when they are fully ripened on the plant itself. This gives us a fullness of what he created for it to give us. When we harvest fruits and vegetables before they're ripe we lose essential phytochemicals.

A phytochemical is the part of the plant that helps them resist fungi, bacteria, and plant virus infections. It also helps the plant reduce bugs and other animals from eating the plant. It only develops at the very last ripening stage of the fruits or vegetables while on the plant. The body needs them to stay healthy.

Picking green and unripe plants makes shipping easier, but makes us weak, tired, and sick. We also lose a *lot* of the flavor. We should use all these things with prudence and a thankful heart. We should take good care of the animals and plants with which we have been so blessed. We should eat them in their proper timing to grow and in the completion of their seasons.

We know that too much meat is a problem for human beings. Our bodies are not designed to consume large quantities of it. Too much meat can cause aggression problems. It affects hormones, moods, and actions. Some people need to eat more meat than others due to constitutional differences and digestion. For most people it is a benefit to have at least a little bit of meat in the diet. Some people can get by without consuming hardly any, but in my experience, that is not recommended for most people. It depends on the person's physical constitution. It seems the body has a difficult time with meat during the hot season when everyone is in the habit of barbecues. You may notice the sluggish feeling you get after eating a lot of barbecued meat in the summer. This is your body signaling it is overtaxed and that heat and meat are not a beneficial combination.

A person's muscle tissue reveals a lot about their dietary needs. Massage is effective in helping to find imbalances and correcting them. There are many types of massage that focus on diet and balance of the constitutional types. When the body runs smooth, strength returns, the mind clears, and the spirit hums. Mind, body, and spirit - all three interconnected. You cannot affect one without affecting the other two.

Grains and fruits and vegetables are very good for the body. Some digest slower and some go faster, creating different kinds of energy for us. A can assist you in knowing what you should or should not eat for your specific needs and what you hope to do. Foods have varying degrees of acidity and alkalinity on top of the speed of digestion. There are also considerations of ionic and anionic foods. These topics are too detailed to cover in this book but you should know that they exist and are vital to health. Seek a professional who understands them. Some foods should never be consumed but used on the outside of the body because they are so strong. Many people consume things for reasons they don't even understand. They eat things for benefits they believe they are getting but that may actually do more harm than good.

Coffee is one of the foods that should *never* be consumed. It's bad for you! I can always tell a person who chooses to drink coffee, even if they don't tell me. Even if they don't smell like it or have stained teeth, I can tell. Whenever I work on their feet there's a particular area that is full of crunchy, hard crystals. The more damaging coffee is to that person's constitution, the more crystals they get. It never ceases to amaze my clients that I can tell that from their foot or how much that area hurts while I work on it. More incredible is when they cut back or completely stop drinking it, and the crystals disappear. Their feet don't hurt anymore! I've even had clients report that ulcers quit bothering them.

If we are going through a healing process we need extra support beyond what only foods can provide for us. Food-based supplements can be lifesavers after getting lots of good, nutrient rich foods. We need a wide variety of colors to support our constitutional needs. But wait! - not all vitamins and minerals are created equal. Most vitamins sold in stores and filled with things your body can't even process or break down. You need the help of a professional to find your way through this. Medical doctors are *not* the ones to talk to about nutrition. They can help you with the interference of your medications, but that's about it in regards to nutrition.

Work with a nutritionist, naturopathic doctor, or someone with a lot of knowledge about food and the body. Not even all massage therapists are trained in nutritional practice. Make sure to ask questions. Medical doctors are great at diagnosing, prescribing drugs, and operating, are outside their scope of practice about nutrition. No one thinks to have someone educated in building health help them because they're misled to go to a doctor for everything.

Do not rely on doctors as your first go-to person to improve your nutrition. Go to a nutritionist, a naturopathic doctor or someone skilled with food and the effects on the body. I've had some excellent doctors do a few surgeries for me and some good friends who are medical doctors. Can't say too much good about the things they helped me with, and many are good people and want to help people. No matter how great all that is you wouldn't take your car to an ice cream shop for repairs, would you? Don't go to a medical doctor for nutrition.

If you have a health issue, something to consider is the timing of onset, your thoughts, and toxicity. Often through massage therapy, we can trace back to when the onset occurred. There is usually an emotional trigger. As time progresses without resolving the issue, it turns into a physical problem. Most people are familiar with diagnosed medical conditions. The body is very intelligent and will do anything to survive, and that includes doing some calculated harm to itself at times to get your attention.

Our body is gives us feedback on the status of how everything is running at all times. The brain will shut down pain signals after a while to conserve energy if we ignore them. It is very efficient that way. The body will make several attempts to get our attention. It will try to auto-correct the problem first. Then, it will try using other resources available within it until it comes full cycle. Once it has used up every resource, we are in big trouble. If we have not listened and made the necessary corrections, it creates a symptom. These increase to symptoms and diseases that are no longer unnoticeable. If we *still* persist in ignoring the body signals we will die.

I'm not saying symptoms are not real. I am not saying people don't get physical diseases that are only that - a physical disease. This does happen sometimes. I'm saying that a lot of times, it starts with emotions. When it does, the emotions must also be addressed.

I relate the story of a client who developed a very deadly disease. (I have changed identifying details to protect his identity.) It was a terrifying experience for him to receive a life threatening diagnosis. When we discussed his medical history, we talked about his life before the diagnosis. He had to think about it for a while. He realized there was a very stressful situation at one of his previous places of employment. He had a new manager who did not treat him with respect even though he performed his job very well. He'd had no problems with the previous managers. He had received a lot of company-wide recognition for his work and got several bonuses.

Cancer is often associated with anger. People react to different things in different ways. This man's illness had been caused by the anger seed decades ago. Realizing this experience was connected to his health situation was a huge breakthrough for him. Once he was able to remember it and realize he still felt angry and hurt about it, he was able to work on letting his anger go. Even though he no longer worked there years later, he was able to forgive the manager for treating him that way. He was also able to forgive *himself* for being so angry and hard on himself. Once he made this change, his cancer took a turn for the better. He is now free of his diagnosed illness. He's also free of the negative effects of that original experience.

Massage helps you become more aware of what is going on inside of your body. It helps you become more in touch with your physical, mental, and spiritual self. Massage can help you undo hurt that has been done. It can help you let go of the past and it can help you move forward to create a wonderful present. All we have is *today*. Massage can help us learn to make the most of it and stay present. If we get rid of the load we have been lugging around, we only have to worry about maintaining our balanced state. That is a lot less work and much more rewarding.

Food is a very powerful thing. It can take us back to a wonderful, fond memory or a terrifying association. Food can make us strong and healthy, or food can make us sick. There are lots of ways it can do both. Something massage taught me is that various things cause different types of allergies. They can be to things, foods, experiences, and even people. When we were in school I recall the day we studied about allergies. I looked up the definition. There was a whole paragraph listing things that cause allergies. One was pollen, but it was farther down the list. One of the most surprising things to me was *anger*. There were a lot of things I'd never heard of associated to allergies in that medical dictionary. All I had heard about was pollen and pets. I stopped dead on the word *anger* and wondered how it could be. I wanted answers.

Since that day I have studied more about allergies and food allergies. There are huge correlations between allergies we develop and emotions - anger more than anything. I have experienced food allergies created by traumatic events. They were able to be permanently removed - without drugs. Dermatologists have diagnosed people having such bad allergies they'd have to receive lifetime shots. The shots would have to be specially formulated for every change of season. Yet these allergies were removed through therapeutic bodywork sessions.

If you're eating or digesting and trauma strikes, the body believes the nutrients are a threat. That's a lot of different nutrients your body is going to think are dangerous. It's not going to be absorbing things properly anymore even though it may be good, healthy food. Not absorbing nutrients makes you malnourished whether you are under or overweight. It can be devastating to your mind and body and can even be deadly.

The third chapter covers myalgic encephalomyelitis. It is also known as chronic fatigue syndrome. (I have learned some secrets for overcoming this syndrome, but more about that some other time.) Food allergies worsened my condition as I became very ill, and as the condition worsened the allergies grew worse. We worked hard at eliminating toxins in my body. I removed inflammatory foods related to the food allergies. We also did various types of bodywork to help me start to come out of it.

There *is* help out there. You can get rid of allergies, contrary to what the medical industry believes. But it cannot be done through medical means. It has to be done through natural methods and the proper bodywork. You have to have a good practitioner who knows what they are doing. What is causing your allergies will determine what you will need to do. Allergies can be based on emotion, trauma, chemical sensitivities, toxins, pollen and other things. There are several modalities that can be very helpful.

While healing and creating balance with food, avoid genetically modified organisms (GMOs). These have been found to be very harmful to the body as they are grown with built-in pesticides. They do not help your wellbeing or physical health. Pesticides are designed to kill. Again, I speak from personal experience. Read the labels when you buy things at the store and know what each of those things mean. "Natural flavors" does *not* mean the flavors from the natural food were used to make it tasty. That's another name for MSG which is known to be addictive and has also been shown to be associated with cancer. There are many other things you have to become familiar with on the labels. *Do your research* about labels today. A lot of dangers hide on them.

Buy the best organic heirloom non-GMO foods you can get. I know some stores flat out lie about their produce. If you can grow your own, that is even better. At least then you will know what is going into them. Be actively involved in your local community governments. Pass and support laws that support smaller farms and businesses. Study the effects of sugar, GMO foods, and pesticides on the body. You might survive on college food and microwaved noodles for a time but you won't *thrive*. The same is true of food that is not real food. Learn to create balanced meals and get help where needed. There are many experts in this field, and it doesn't take too long to learn these things. Once you have, teach your family and friends. Sharing is caring.

To enrich and fatten up our bone marrow we need dark leafy greens. We need yams, bone broth, and fresh fruits and vegetables. We need a variety of unadulterated whole grains prepared in unique ways. These are the things that give us richness in our bones, strength, and gut health. The topic of *food* is too wide and deep to cover in such a small book as this one. It is so very important to learn though. Learn to eat the way your body needs to eat; that honors it. It will, in turn, give you strength, understanding, and the ability to do the things you dream of doing.

Beware of diets. Diets almost always create imbalance, regardless of results. They also create a sense of nutritional insecurity in your body. Diets give temporary results, but not long lasting ones. They create so much stress on the body that it is forced to compensate. Dieting shocks the body and creates a yo-yo effect - where you lose weight and then gain it back again. This is devastating and does not get the end results you're after, which is why you have to diet again and again.

Learning to do things right in baby steps is the best way to go. Baby steps help you learn to be healthy and look and feel good for the long term. First, honor that you are not someone else. Be okay with having a different body type, constitution, or drive than someone else. What you have is already amazing and admirable. Learn to see that about yourself so you can embrace it. What you have is better and unique. You need *your* body's owner's manual - not someone else's - if you're not where you want to be right now. Be willing to be the best *you*, whatever that means for you, that you can be. Once you can do that, you will shine in a way that only you can. People will be in awe of you, and, most of all, you will be too!

I can't tell you how many clients come into my office with some kind of perceived body issue. Most of them don't even realize it. I know I sure didn't. Everyone thinks that everyone else has a perfect body. *Everyone* has scars and stretchmarks and a lot of the other things that you worry about with your body too.

The amazing thing about massage is that it helps you think about yourself in a loving way, scars and all. Instead of judging ourselves by impossible social standards, we find our own true beauty. We see our own true worth. Mirrors, magazines, television, and society are not very accurate at representing a *real* body in a positive light. Even our own eyes can deceive us based on false perceptions. My clients come to see their own beauty and worth through bodywork. Once they do, they make even more progress towards their other goals!

Page 154

One of the most important things you can do is to eat the right food for your body in the right combinations and correct order. This is essential to support your body's needs and requirements for optimal function. Food can be delicious and enjoyable when eating the right things in the right way. Be patient with yourself.

Different things in the body can greatly affect your taste buds. This influences how everything will taste to you. Some of these things include parasites, tapeworms, fungus, and candida. Also how acidic or alkaline you are, the toxins and heavy metals in your body, and medications you may take – all these things can affect the taste of food. Flavor perception *can* be changed and it will affect the way things taste to you. You may find the foods you previously hated before actually become foods you love.

Proper food use is a big learning curve for many people. Often, we learn bad eating habits from our families, but if we learn to eat better it can change our lives. Remember: we do the best we can with what we currently know. It is in our best interest to always be advancing our knowledge and moving forward in life.

Some body types do fine on only two or three meals a day. Others have to have three meals and snacks daily to barely make it through the day. They may even have to keep a snack near their bed at night. Some people need lots of healthy fats in their diets, and for others it is very harmful to have much fat in their diets. It is important to understand your own body. Even the fact that you are in the same family does not mean that you will have the same constitution and nutritional needs.

We can't eat just anything and everything and expect it to give us an equal amount of energy as everything else. Live foods give us the most *bang* for our buck. If it takes organs forty units to break down food and you eat something that only gives you five units of energy, you're going to run out of energy pretty fast! You're not going to lose or gain weight by doing that, either, if that's one of your goals; you will lose your health. Instead, eat foods that give back as close to the forty units that it takes to break down the food - or more. This will allow you to at least maintain your wellness. A fresh cucumber will have a very high energy producing level, as high as forty units. A cheeseburger from a fast food restaurant might be closer to five units - or even *negative* five. If you eat in a deficit, you will lose energy. There are some wonderful books that go into lots of detail about these things. If you get overwhelmed with all the information, I recommend asking for help.

No one of us can be an expert at everything. Be good at something, and do it well. My intent is to touch on a few things to get you thinking about where you are at now. I encourage you to take action today on building your own wellness. Almost everyone I've ever met has *some* type of food issue in their life. A couple familiar ones include equating food to love or not having enough food to begin with. There are many others, and I could go on all day about the many mistaken perceptions people have about food. This does *not* make us bad people.

It's just something to be aware of that we can change so we have a better relationship with our food. It's easy to turn your metaphorical steering wheel to make a U-turn with a little help from someone who is trained to walk you through it.

SECTION 3
EXERCISE

EXERCISE is a very important topic and there is usually a lot of charged emotion around it. A lot of people hate doing it, while at the other end of the spectrum there are some people who seem to enjoy springing out of bed to go work out. There is a reason for this wide range of sentiment about exercise. There are different physical constitutions. Some people are naturally light and moving all the time. Exercise gives them energy to move. Others are more inclined to solid stability and groundedness. These are both good and challenge us in different ways. Both types can benefit each other if they are willing to work together. Both types can also be harmed by too much of their own constitution or by too much of another's.

Different kinds of people have different movement needs. There are also various levels and types of exercise. A well-trained massage therapist can help you determine your type and what is best for your body's needs. This can change over time, especially if you have an imbalance one way or another. Food, water, and other necessary intake levels will change as you come into balance and harmony or go out of it.

Movement is essential for all types of people. The lymphatic system is a part of the circulation and immune systems. Its main focus is to return escaped fluids and proteins to the cells and tissues in the body. It removes cellular debris, things that don't belong there, and works with the immune response to help keep us healthy. Good to know: it helps clean the inside of the body, but is only able to function when you are moving. It's kind of like the recycler and cleanup man of the blood stream.

There are little sections of lymph in different areas of the body. If you want your body to be clean inside, you have to get the lymph working, so get your body moving.

People have different needs, and there are lots of ways to move to achieve a person's goals. Some people may only need fifteen minutes of light movement a day to be fit; more than that would overexert their system. Some people will need an hour of movement a day to get their engines started. They have so much strength and power inside them that it takes a little longer to get their system warmed up and going. Don't expect yourself to have to keep up with someone else and don't expect less of yourself than what you need. Don't underestimate what you can do.

If you want to reach a goal, first make sure it's a healthy one *for you*. Make sure it's within your reach. Once you've done that, set proper limits that you will stay within, and then push yourself to reach those goals. Like in the story "Broken" (Chapter 2) and having to learn how to walk all over again, don't ever give up. Keep pushing yourself. It may take a lot of time and effort. Sometimes you may have to adjust your goal as you go along but you can do anything you set your mind to doing.

One of my clients had settled into a bit of depression because she had gone through several difficult trials in her life. She started coming in for massage and sometimes she talked about how she used to love dancing. She used to teach a particular style of dancing. I asked her why she stopped and why she didn't pick it up again if she loved it so much. After a few more sessions and similar conversations, she came into the office one day beaming. She had started dancing again, and she was so happy. She said that it was the best thing she ever did for herself.

Find something that you enjoy doing that brings you joy and the results you want. For some people that will look like ballet, swimming, or yoga. For others it will look like weight lifting and cycling. For still others it could look like running or kayaking. Something beneficial for almost everyone is walking; it benefits the entire body, and there are fun things you can do to make it more interesting. You can do certain breathing exercises while you walk, or play your favorite music. Make things fun and customize your exercise to yourself and take a buddy along. It's easier and more exciting to have someone to talk to and push you to keep going - and you can do the same for them. The most important thing is to *get moving*. When you quit moving you start dying, so move and live!

SECTION 4
SLEEP

SLEEP is another area that gets overlooked and far too often underrated. When you get a therapeutic massage or other type of bodywork, you may experience falling asleep. You may get very close to falling asleep as you achieve a deep state of relaxation. Not too often, sometimes people will even fall completely asleep.

When the body is processing data and experiences, our subconscious mind is being accessed. Much like a computer, the subconscious sorts through the files and decides what needs to be tossed out. We do most of our processing when we are asleep. Sometimes an opportunity arises to decide where some unfiled things need to go in our minds. Other times, people fall asleep, because they have a sleep deficit and are really overworked and tired. Sleeping is a vital part of bodywork and it is vital to healing our body, our mind, and our spirit.

Getting a massage is not the only time our body needs to sleep and process things. Our bodies love structure and stability. A few of us thrive on unpredictability and randomness, but at the core, we still do best if we have our basics covered on a very predictable timetable. As an example, the body loves to go to bed at the same time and wake up at the same time every single day. The body also loves it when we eat our meals at the same time every day. The physical body loves consistency the same way plants do. Learn about and understand the way melatonin works with a regular sleep cycle - it helps us get into that deep sleep at night. We sleep best when it is dark outside to go along with our own body's circadian rhythm.

The hours that we sleep before midnight are much more beneficial for us. I have learned every hour of sleep that you get before midnight is like two hours after midnight to the body. Don't take my word for it, though; try it out and see for yourself. Try it for a month both ways; go to bed and wake up at different times every day for a month – stay up late and go to bed early, sleep in and get up early. Then for one month try going to bed at nine or ten in the evening and getting up at six in the morning every day. See which one leaves you feeling better.

Another aspect of sleep is taking naps. Kids need naps because they are growing so fast, and the body grows while sleeping. Naps allow the body to recharge and refresh. The lighter, higher movement constitution like vata needs to take naps during the day. They use up so much energy with all the bouncing off the walls they do. You may notice mid-day – 2:00 p.m. to 4:00 p.m. a feeling of exhaustion. This is the best time for those with lighter constitutions to slow down and take a break, do nothing, and even sleep.

For the more solid, strong types of constitutions, it is vital to move. This type of person's strength and stability can create stagnation without it. Movement is essential to avoid sluggishness and feeling stuck. Keep things moving. Whichever type you are, if you honor strengths and take care of weaknesses, your health will be better, and you will feel happier.

The hardest thing to do is to do the right thing for *your* body and not the right thing for someone else. I know: it goes against everything society teaches. Society says there should be one good thing that works for everyone. Doing the right thing for your own body goes against what you are used to doing, to get through life every day. As you truer to yourself, others will like the changes they see. They'll ask you what you've been doing. Be careful not to confuse your true self with the act of rebelling against someone else's idea of you or who you think, they think, you are.

Getting enough sleep reduces stress. It helps us feel more relaxed, like eating the right foods does. The more we can allow and accept our own needs and requirements, the more we can make room for others. We can allow that their needs are different than ours, and *that's okay*. We all balance each other out but we also need the differences we all have to contribute to the greater whole. As we learn better ways to do things, we pass that knowledge on, and then all of society is affected for the better.

SECTION 5
STRETCHING

ONE OF MY FAVORITE THINGS about massage is the amount of stretching we do with the muscles. Most people do not exercise or stretch. People who exercise at all usually only exercise, skipping an important step: stretching. Some people get plenty of exercise from their normal everyday routines. If we don't stretch things out, we start to see shorter muscles full of knots, soreness, and stiffness. Left unchecked, this leads to compression of the joints, which can wear out the cartilage faster. When cartilage wears out, the bones rub on each other, something that's very painful. The pain can make it difficult to walk, stand, open doors, and fasten buttons. People in this situation may get arthritis and need a hip replacement or knee surgery.

The body stores information inside itself about trauma, stress, and other things. Stretching can help to ease some of these anxieties from our lives. Yoga is a great way to stretch, but not all yoga is the same. If it is done right and is the right kind of flow for stretching, it should never leave you feeling like you worked out. A good yoga session is performed between a place of effort and relaxation so that you feel like you are floating. This takes time to learn how to do it right and requires much practice. When you are done, you should feel relaxed, at peace, and limber. If you do yoga every day, you only need a fifteen-to-twenty minute session each day.

When I first started learning yoga, it took me about a year before I felt comfortable with it. It took a long time before I felt like I was doing it right. At first, I had reservations about *ever* doing it, but it got to the point that I had to try it because of the results I needed. I was not disappointed.

Now I am a strong advocate of a good yoga flow for my clients. It makes the results of their massage sessions last longer. They feel much better between appointments. Usually, a person will feel good after a massage for a day or two, but if they do yoga every day, the benefits of the massage could last a week or two. I even had one client tell me that he felt amazing for an entire month when doing yoga daily. He couldn't say enough good things about the massage and especially the yoga. He loved that he was able to do the yoga in the comfort of his home because it saved him time, money, and was so convenient.

Although, it is incredible, yoga is not for everyone. There are other types of stretching that you can do. For example: proprioceptive neuromuscular facilitation (PNF Stretching) is one of the most effective forms of stretching. But, it requires someone trained in the modality to help you. It uses a combination of active and passive stretching and movement. It is great for strengthening weak areas and lengthening areas that are too strong. Often, professional athletes use both methods of stretching – yoga and PNF stretching - due to how well they work.

If you do *any* type of repetitive motion with your body for employment, you classify as an athlete. Your need for athletic stretching is vital in order to avoid injuring yourself. If you don't stretch regularly, you will very likely develop imbalances within your body and that can lead to injury.

Injuries can lead to necessary surgeries. They can lead to needing to replace joints and cartilage. For every hour of physical exertion you do, you should do at least a half hour of stretching of those same muscles. Stretching before *and* after a workout is important. If you only have time to do one or the other, stretching *after* exercising or working will give you a greater stretch. The fascia layers (body sock holding the muscle bundles together) will be warmed up and they will stretch farther afterward. But, it is no substitute for stretching before *and* after. Stretch, get a massage, or do both.

SECTION 6 RECEIVING MASSAGE

NOT EVERYONE has enough time to stretch and/or exercise every day. Our culture is always in such a rush, and we each have many things to do all the time. The stress builds and the pressure mounts. We find ourselves cutting people off on the roadway or yelling at the kids. We yell at each other and hate our lives. We may hate other people who seem happy and feel like we are going to burst. Then, we develop health issues on top of everything else we have going on. We don't seem to have time to slow down, so we push on - and it gets worse and worse.

Proper hydration and eating nutrient-dense foods promote wellness. We need proper sleep habits, good activities, and rest. All these things help us keep our life in a state of balance. When we don't take - or make - time to do the things we need to restore what we have lost, we begin to die a slow, painful death. Massage therapy is a very good solution to these problems. Massage helps remind us to take care of what we have, much like taking our cars in for a checkup. It's like going in to the doctor for an annual exam.

A good massage therapist has training in nutrition, body psychology, anatomy, and neurology. These subjects help the massage therapist understand how bones, nerves, and muscles interact through various modalities and allow them to be able to put things into a better working order for you. The therapist may specialize in physical or energy massage. Remember: you cannot affect the physical body without affecting the energy of the body, and vice versa. If the therapist has a working understanding of both, they will possibly be much better at what they do. It also helps them know where their working boundaries are and when you may need someone else to step in and help. Not everyone does the same thing and not everyone knows the same things.

There are hundreds of different types of massage work you can receive. Each type will have a various effects on different people with the same modality due to their different constitutions. Experiment a little with different types of massage. Become familiar with the benefits and how your body reacts to them. What works amazingly for one person may be a very bad idea for someone else. Take into account your life trauma, medical history, and physical and emotional aptitudes. Also make sure to look at the therapist giving the treatment.

As all treatments are not equal, not all therapists are, either. Like in any industry, there are good ones and bad ones. You will find those who are highly skilled and those who are not. You will find those with many years of experience and those who are new and starting out. Massage is a very hands-on industry, and so skill level must be hand tested. Try out several therapists until you find the one that is right for you.

If you use massage on your wellness journey, you may find you need a few different therapists to help you. Your needs may change as you get into deeper layers of emotion and trauma that you want to clear out. One therapist may have a skill set that will take you only so far. Another may have different skills to round out what you need. Be glad to have so many people who can help you! We may be sad to see you go for a while until you need us again, but we're happy for your progress. We also wish you the best in your journey.

Picking a massage therapist is like looking for a new pair of shoes: you have to try a lot of them. You want to find a pair that fits well, doesn't pinch or make you feel uncomfortable, and feels right. You always have the right to change your mind *without explanation.*

This next topic I approach with the kindest, most sensitive instruction: bathe before you go to receive a massage. Don't assume the therapist won't mind. You want your body to be clean, whether you get a clothed modality or disrobe. If you disrobe, you will be under a sheet and a towel or blanket at all times. Only the section of your body that is being worked on is uncovered, and then it is covered up again.

Most therapists don't care if you shave, wear makeup, or even get all dressed-up - as long as you aren't dirty. If you can, it's better to show up without makeup and wear comfortable clothing. You may have your face down in the face rest for a while and all your makeup will rub off anyway. If you don't have makeup on, it's easier to launder the sheets too. Massage oil or lotion is difficult to get out as it is; some makeup *never* comes out and then the therapist has to toss the face rest cover altogether.

Sometimes people cry during a massage as emotions are gently released. If you're wearing it, crying will make your makeup run. You may end up looking like the matchmaker in the movie *Mulan* after Mulan goes to see her to find a husband. Most of the time, clients often don't expect to be crying or uncontrollably laughing, but they sometimes do.

We know as therapists that crying or laughing is going to occur sometime or another. We understand, and we still think you are beautiful. We've experienced this emotional trauma release ourselves, including the running mascara! We have seen it so much that its standard operating procedure for us. We know that once you let those feelings go that you will feel much better. We *want* that for you.

Comfortable clothing is easier to change out of if you disrobe, easier to move in if you get a clothed modality, and won't get ruined by the oils we may use if you're wearing fine fabrics. Oil is difficult to wash out, so be mindful of what you wear for your appointment. After your massage appointment you may feel so relaxed that struggling with buttons and zippers is not what you will want to be doing. Sometimes you have to get back to work though, so do what you need to do.

The massage therapist you have spent the time to find will get very close to you in your personal space. You trust this person to work on you, so make their job easier and more pleasant by showing up *clean*. It makes us very happy, and makes our job easier.

Don't show up with unwashed feet or dirty clothes and smelly socks. Showing up clean shows respect for yourself, your goals, and your therapist. If it can't be avoided, bring some wipes with you to clean your feet and body odor before your appointment. Wash up in the bathroom beforehand.

The therapist may not work on you or even accept you as a client if you go in dirty or smelling bad. It can actually be a work hazard for your therapist - and a safety hazard for their other clients - if you are not washed. They will thank you for taking the time and making the effort on their behalf to be clean. They have made a large effort to make their space clean, safe, and comfortable for you. By coming in clean, you help them maintain it that way for others as well.

Part of getting a massage is cleaning out all the stuff inside that has become stagnant and stuck in the body. The skin is an elimination organ, and therapists have to work through it to get to the deeper layers of muscle and bone. The skin can't do its job and the massage strokes won't work well if there isn't a clean surface to work with. Think of your body as a piece of art and the therapist as an artist. Your body should be a blank canvas to work with so they can create a masterpiece.

Before your massage appointment, make sure you are well hydrated. This helps the fluids in your body move the stagnant acids and toxins in your body to its disposal units. Hydration helps your tissues relax easier. It also helps the therapist by allowing them to use less oil on you. Too much oil leaves you greasy - not to mention it makes the laundry harder to do. Having enough fluids in your body can help prevent you from having headaches. It can help you avoid feeling flu-like symptoms when all the toxins are flushing through your body on their way out. If you feel this way, you should drink more water. The therapist should instruct you on proper water intake after the massage.

Expect the therapist to explain what their process is. They should tell you what to expect to happen to you before, during, and after bodywork. If you are not comfortable with anything they tell you, *tell them* what you are not comfortable with. A good therapist won't ever do anything to make you feel uncomfortable but you have to *let them know*. Of course, you are free to leave or change your mind about letting them work on you at any time *without explanation*. Report any misconduct to the authorities. No one should ever touch any of your private areas during a massage or work under the sheet. (You should never request it, either.) No reputable therapist will *ever* do anything like that. If they do, report them to the local state massage licensing board and the police.

Your job during a massage is to relax and enjoy the work being done. Some modalities have you move around and help the therapist. Your therapist will explain the process to you before and during the session. Throughout the massage, stay in good, open communication with the therapist.

Tell them how the pressure feels or if any pressure is deep enough that you have to tighten up any part of your body. Even if it feels good to tighten up, you shouldn't. This is a sign from your body that the pressure is too deep, even if it doesn't hurt. You may want lighter or heavier pressure.

Feeling ticklish is a sign that you have a buildup of toxins in that area. It will need extra work to get them cleared out. A good massage is not always full of tingling and goosebumps - that is another sign of excess toxins building up in the system that will need working out.

If an area feels like "heaven with a cherry on top" good, let your therapist know. This is another sign of excess toxins in the area. Staying in close communication with your therapist will result in a better massage. Communication allows them to make necessary adjustments designed especially for you. Each person has very different things that they like. Don't be afraid to let the therapist know if they are doing something that doesn't feel good to you. One client might love a certain technique and the next client might hate it. The therapist won't be offended in the least if you tell them to try something different. You may even decide on a different day that you want to try out the same technique you hated three months ago again. It happens often.

After your massage, take your time getting up. Make sure that you are grounded and can feel the floor balanced beneath your feet. Do not try to get up if you feel light headed or floaty; you need to be grounded better first. If you had a disrobed massage, get dressed again. Your therapist will remind you of the homework you need to do until your next appointment. Be sure to follow their directions to the letter!

I can always tell when my clients have not iced after they go home. I can also tell if they've done their stretches or not and if they done their assigned activities. It shows up in the way their tissue feels, and there is no way to fake that. I give my clients one chance not to do their homework if they want me to keep working on them.

Massage in its intended form is not a one-sided activity. It takes my doing my part to help you move forward. It takes your doing your part during the week to hold your place with where we got you to at your last visit. Together we can do so much. A massage where you don't do anything on your part or a massage done infrequently is a luxury experience. The benefits will only last a day or two, and then they're gone. You will lose any positive results from which you could have benefited.

Massage therapy can be a preventative treatment for medicine, chiropractic care, and other types of therapy. I have specialized in the more clinical types of massage, a lot of which is aimed at preventing surgeries or recovery from surgery or automobile accidents. The work I attract is for people who are trying to heal their body, mind, and spirit. Often, they have already tried medicine and other routes without success. Some have not been able to find a diagnosis for what has been troubling them. Some are lucky enough that massage is their first stop.

We need to get in the habit of helping our bodies first by natural means, when things are in the early stages, before things get so bad. Turning to chemicals and surgeries as a primary solution to health problems is backwards thinking. Our society is starting to realize this and make changes in the way it thinks as a whole. More people are turning to preventative care as a first course of action. I'm excited about where we are going.

I hope this chapter helps you think about things and take inventory of how they're working for you. Ask yourself if it is possible for things to work better and if you are willing to *let them*. The first step is the hardest; then, you have to keep going and not give up.

SECTION 7 SERVING OTHERS

WHEN WE FEEL DOWN and like life is too much to bear, it can be easy to feel sorry for ourselves. It's tempting to close ourselves off from the rest of the world. We may indulge in food and behaviors that harm us even further. This starts a downward spiral and we begin to feel worse and worse as time goes by. It seems like sometimes the things that are best for us are the most difficult to do. If we can catch ourselves early in the process, we can reverse our choices. Then, we learn to catch ourselves more quickly until we change our habits completely. We never have to head down the dark hole of despair again unless we forget our good habits.

Looking outside of ourselves and our troubles is a way to forget our worries and focus on someone else. This may help us realize that others may have a worse situation to deal with than we do. Helping those people makes us feel needed and useful. We get a sense of accomplishment. It picks up our emotions when we are able to do even the smallest thing for someone who cannot help themselves.

Groups in your community have needs and pray for help. Go to your local church group and ask who in the congregation needs help. Search online to find community service organizations. There are websites like https://justserve.org, where people and organizations put what they need help with. Pick something that interests you and help. For every skill set, you will find something you can most likely do. Go by yourself, go with a friend, or get a group of people together and go. Try out different things to find what you enjoy and about which you feel passionate.

The more you help others, the better you will feel, though you may have delayed gratification so keep going. It is difficult to help someone without feeling compassion and love for them. The more good things you do for others, the better you will feel. Love casts out depression, fear, and a whole slew of other things that drag us down.

If you have a severe condition in "Deep Sleep" (Chapter 3), you may not feel like there is anything you can do for anyone else. But remember that you can let people know you are ill so *they* have the option to support *you*. When I got chronic fatigue, I thought I would never be free of it. There was so much not known about it, but I finally overcame it. I found a way out. If you do the work, you can make it through your trial too, even if it seems long. If you can handle having a friend come over or your family to help you, you will better know that you are needed and loved.

For example, you can try to color a very small picture. Then, a loved one can use the picture to make a "get well" card for someone they know who needs cheering up. You can listen to a young child read a story to you. Collect ideas online of the things you would like to do for someone once you are feeling stronger. Sometimes you need to rest and recover, and *that is okay*. If you can muster up the energy, do something good for someone else. You'll be glad you did. Helping others is one of the best ways you can start to help yourself.

One of the reasons I love massage and bodywork so much is that I get to help people who want help. I get to see instant results - and so do they. Who doesn't love seeing instant improvement? I'm very blessed to be a massage therapist and bodyworker; to be entrusted with that kind of care for another human being is very rewarding for both the client and me. To love what you do is one of life's greatest rewards. I can think of no greater thing to do in life than to help people get to the point where *they* love what *they* do. Do what you're passionate about!

SECTION 8
FINDING
RESOURCES

FINDING RESOURCES is easier in some areas than others. Word of mouth is a good place to start. People love to talk about their favorite massage therapist, or keep them a complete secret because they don't want to have to fight for appointments. If the therapist is good, everyone wants to see them. If you are lucky enough to be in a town that doesn't mind sharing and networking, then word of mouth is a fabulous way to go. People living in small towns tend to know everyone and all about each other. They're usually willing to tell you who is good at what they do and who not to go to.

Larger cities have more resources and variety. There are so many options and willingness to network that you can get lost. If you find good groups set up for this purpose, you may be rewarded with some good connections. Those of you who know me know how much I love puns and happy little ironies. I just realized in the hundredth edit that this is section 8. (Laugh with me if you figure it out!) I didn't know this book was going to have a bunch of patterns and puzzles in it too. It's like a "Where's Waldo?" game.

The internet is a great resource to use to research massage therapists and find further resources. Many massage therapists want to help you get your body natural and balanced. Here are some things that may benefit you. Your local therapist may know of other things specific to your area that may not be on this list:

The National Certification Board of Therapeutic Massage and Bodywork (NCBTMB) is a national certification board for massage therapists. The link below will help you find a therapist who is nationally and/or board certified in your area. The extra training required for either of these certifications is worth your time to research: https://www.ncbtmb.org/tools/find-a-certified-massage-therapist

The NCBTMB website will take you to a page where you can find massage therapists by *state licensing requirements:* https://www.ncbtmb.org/regulators/state-info

Online, there are websites for many different types of massage modalities. There are *hundreds* of types of massage. There are quite a few massage modalities where you remain fully clothed. I will not list the types of practice available to you in this book because it would become too exhaustive.

Research naturopathic and functional medicine doctors, chiropractors, nutritionists, and personal trainers. Look for people with a focus in natural, gentle, healing methods. These specialists can help point you in the right direction of other people who can also help you. They should be willing to work with each other and together with you for your best outcome. They should also know more what's available in your local areas, and if they don't, try someone else.

Get a good diagnosis from *more than one person*. You need to know what is going on with your body. Then go to the person(s) who have the specializations to help you reach your goal. Just because someone diagnoses you does not mean you have to let them treat you. You can have someone else help you or even several people, and *that's okay*. Talk to someone who has a lot of experience in their field, which can be helpful in finding good resources. Talking to many different specialists will provide you with even more resources.

It takes work to reclaim wellness. Remember: it took time to get where you are, and it will take time to get back out of it. *You* decide what the best course of action for you will be. No one person or group is going to have all the answers. You will need a team of people, so look for the best people that are available to you. It's in your best interests and is the best use of your resources.

SECTION 9
BALANCE

SOME PEOPLE think of balance as a scale with a fixed point in the middle that never moves. The focal point is in the middle and always stays in the middle. The definition of balance is a state of equilibrium. It is characterized by the canceling out of all forces by opposing forces equal in nature. Equality for the body does not mean that all the sides have the same amount of space around the focal point. It means that there is an equal amount of force. Which weighs more, a ton of feathers or a ton of bricks? The answer is: they weigh the same. They both weigh a ton. (You would definitely have a much larger pile of feathers than you would bricks, but they weigh the same.)

Each person requires a different amount of applied force to create balance. This is based on where levels for things in their life and wellness are and how they affect them. Balance, like feathers and bricks, will look different from one person to another. This is a good thing, and we should embrace this in our personal lives, our family's lives, and in society.

Balance is also known as the power or means to decide. When we don't make active choices that keep our opposing forces in check, our lives become imbalanced. It is easy to grab a burger and plop onto the couch after work, tired from a long day, but these are not choices that will keep our bodies in harmony and balance.

Life requires us to choose things that are often more work, take more thought, and need more effort. This means we have to plan it into our schedule. For some this is not difficult, but for others it is more of a struggle. Your massage therapist may be trained in many different techniques to help you. Together you can create a plan for success. Remember: they are experts at helping you restore balance in your life. If you listen to them, they can help you. All therapists are not trained in the same modalities. You will have to ask what they specialize in or try several therapists out until you find one who can best help you.

Achieving a state of balance can give you more energy to do the things that you want to do. It can help you feel more at peace with yourself, your family, the people you work with, and all other areas of your life. There are so many things that can affect us when we are stressed out. Some of those things are eating an imbalanced diet or not getting enough rest. Having tight muscles or feeling a lot of tension can throw us off balance too. When these areas tax us individually, it wears on our systems. The combined effect can be overwhelming and too much for us to handle. We may start to feel angry and upset over minor things that didn't used to bother us. We feel impatient with those around us. We become frustrated by situations that don't work out the way we had hoped. We find dissatisfaction in everything. Soon, it begins to feed on itself until it takes on a life of its own, and we begin to feel powerless to make any changes.

Asking for help is one of the most difficult things you will ever do. It is also one of the bravest. Facing your own fears is the scariest thing in the world. No one else can scare you more than you. Having the strength and ability to overcome your *self* is the greatest test of willpower. I find it to be one of the most admirable traits in a person: the willingness to face themselves and their own demons. This is the greatest demonstration of true power and strength that you can show.

The most formidable foe is the one who first has conquered self

Once you have conquered yourself, you have no need to act out of fear, lack, guilt, or anger. You also have no need to try to conquer others. There is only balance, peace, love, and harmony. We no longer exist on the end of losing everything we value. We begin existing in a state where we *create* everything that is most important.

Balance is the beginning of all things. It is a doorway to enter, and we must continue along its path, always moving forward. Balance cannot be maintained by remaining still; it was never intended to be so. Balance is ever learning, ever growing, ever progressing day by day. It is not perfection but working towards completion. What that looks like for each individual is going to be different from what it looks like for others. Even identical twins do not have the same balance needs. Their completion picture will be as entirely different and unique as they are.

SECTION 10
MEDITATION

Page 204

MEDITATION is the act of reflecting on something, it is contemplation. It relates to planning in the mind and intention. The mind is trained, calmed, or emptied by focusing on a single object. Meditation has many benefits, all of which are excellent for the body. For example, it boosts the immune system and improves the quality of sleep. It increases our positive emotions while reducing negative ones. It reduces the stress we may feel. Meditation may even be a good antidepressant for depression and help prevent relapses. In the brain, it increases the density of gray matter related to learning and memory. It also affects emotional regulation and empathy. Meditating can teach us how to tune out distractions. It helps improve our memory and attention skills. It even helps with our decision-making.

Those who practice meditation tend to be more compassionate. They think of the needs of others. They are more likely to help people in need. They better understand other people's suffering. Learning compassion for your own self is another benefit. We can *all* use more self-kindness.

Meditation increases our sense of who we are and affects the way we see ourselves. We're more likely to act in line with our own values when we meditate. We have a healthier body image and stronger sense of self-esteem. This is vital in a world of false body image online, in magazines, and in our entertainment. Meditation helps us be more resistant to the negative feedback that is all around us. It helps us be a positive example of healthy body image and self-respect.

One of the great rewards that come from meditation is enhanced relationships. Couples are more satisfied; they feel more relaxed and more optimistic towards themselves and each other. They become more accepting. Because of their ability to get over conflict quicker, they feel closer to one another, and they are often a lot happier than they would otherwise be. I don't think I've ever met anyone who didn't brighten at the idea of being happier.

Parents and parents-to-be can also benefit from meditation. To be successful, they must learn how to reduce the anxiety, depression, and stress they go through. Reducing these levels brings down premature birth risks and developmental problems in children. Parents who meditate have less stress and better relationships with their kids. These parents are able to practice more positive parenting. Kids are less likely to experience depression and anxiety – and will have better social skills in school and at home as they age. When parents are less stressed, they may pay more attention to their kids, and kids love that and thrive. Teens experience less stress and depression. Meditation increases their happiness and self-compassion. For college students, meditation can reduce binge drinking and other risky behaviors.

We are starting to hear a lot more about post-traumatic stress disorder (PTSD) on the news. It's seen in veterans, police officers, and people who have suffered abuse. Even helpful, loving caregivers can experience PTSD. It's thought that training in meditation may be helpful to overcome trauma along with bodywork and massage.

Meditation boosts resilience. In some classrooms they teach meditation to children who now show decreased behavior problems, aggression, and depression and increased happiness. Kids pay more attention to their lessons and the teachers, resulting in teachers' blood pressure being lower. The teachers are more effective and teach with less urgency and distress.

The healthcare and mental health industries likewise benefit. For example, prisoners who practice meditation are less angry and hostile, and there are fewer fights in prison. Meditation also helps in their rehabilitation and reintegration into society.

Bias and prejudices can be reduced and even eliminated with meditation. It's good for business. It makes leaders more confident and creative. It helps people focus on the task at hand rather than trying to do too many things at once. Customers like dealing with more relaxed business people, so *they* are happier.

Meditation even helps fight obesity. Mindful eating and regular massage along with meditation can help people lose weight. They all help them eat less because they feel better and pay more attention to their bodies. They also tend to have healthier babies.

No matter how we regulate our own minds and bodies, with meditation we see relaxation. We see spiritual growth and self-improvement in all areas of our lives. Reaching a meditative state feels peaceful, quiet, and calm. We become more aware of our surroundings. It's a great resource to help us become our best selves. Anyone can use it.

You won't need any drugs to numb your senses once you master meditation. You will achieve the relief you seek using this method. We could all use a little more meditation.

Here are a couple ideas that may help you:

Focus on your breathing. This can help when you are feeling strong emotions to bring you back into self-control. Notice little details about your environment. Can you smell the interior of the building you are in? If you are outside, do you smell the earth, the plants, and the air? What do you notice about them? Pay attention to the things you see and what you notice about them. What do you hear? Are there birds, traffic, the humming of appliances? What qualities do they have? How do these things make you feel as you notice them? Where do you feel these things in your body? Your thoughts and feelings cannot hurt you.

Imagine that you are an alien scientist visiting from another planet, here to do research.

Allow yourself to feel the full size of your emotions as if they were not your own. From an outside perspective and without judgment, feel the physical sensations in your body. Sensations and emotions do not define you. Allow your body to process the experience. Let it file it away where it needs to go or to toss it once it learns what it needs to from that experience. Focus on how your *body* feels. Notice the heat, the blood pulsing through your veins. Feel the movement of the air, the way your body feels against the ground or your chair.

A massage therapist can help you train your mind and get you back in touch with your body. They are there to help you reach your goals using meditation. It can be easy to get stuck with what to do next, especially when you are starting out. You may experience strong emotions or overwhelming sensations. Your therapist can help you work through this in your massage sessions. Eventually you will learn some of these techniques well enough to try them at home. Focused and purposeful meditation can be truly healing for the body, mind, and spirit. It is a great tool.

SECTION 11
LAUGHING

LAUGHTER IS THE BEST remedy. It's not only fun to laugh but it can actually improve your health. Sometimes laughter comes from joyful events and sometimes it comes out of tragedy. It helps us cope with sadness and everyday life. Humor can come from the most unexpected situations and experiences. Here is one such story:

A young, married couple purchased an old farmhouse that had some fruit trees growing on the property. They were delighted to have purchased their first home together. They looked forward with anticipation to the fresh, homegrown produce the next season. They talked to the friendly neighbors, who had lived in the neighborhood for many years, and asked about the property they had purchased and what the yield was like from the trees.

Everything sounded wonderful, except for one tree. There was a cherry tree that was always really wormy every year. The previous owners always had to spray it early in the spring to prevent this. The neighbors recommended tearing out the cherry tree and planting a new one. They warned the young couple several times to be sure to spray the tree every year if they intended to eat the fruit.

The couple was broke after having bought their beautiful new home, so they would not be able to afford to spray the tree that first year. They figured they would see how bad the worm problem was with the cherry tree and spray the next year.

Winter turned to spring and the cherry blossoms were so beautiful and pink. Summer came, green leaves filled in, and soon the cherries started to develop. The husband looked forward with anxious anticipation to tasting those dark, sweet cherries. The wife watched with great reservation as the time went by because she remembered the neighbor's warning.

Finally, the day arrived that the first cherries turned to a deep purple-black color. One morning, the husband and wife were out admiring how the yard was coming along. The husband decided he was going to try those tempting cherries. He declared his intentions, and his wife followed along behind him with words of caution. She reminded him what their kind neighbors had warned them about the previous fall.

Throwing caution to the wind, he waved his wife's warnings away and strode off to the tree with purposeful steps. He plucked a handful of cherries off the tree. He looked at the shiny pristine exteriors. They were plump with enticing goodness and he threw one into his mouth.

His wife cried out in shock and told him not to eat the cherry but to break one open first. He should check the inside before eating them - even just one. The worms would be on the inside, after all. He went on and on about how tasty and delicious the cherry was as he stood proud in the front yard of the farmhouse - his own castle. He was king of the mountain with his cherries.

He proceeded to pop several more cherries into his mouth and chewed with great satisfaction. His wife was about out of her mind, imploring him to check the cherries before he ate them. She thought she might be sick. She had experience with fruit trees and harvesting fruit, and she told him that he was going to regret not checking the cherries first.

He carelessly tossed another few handfuls of the fruit into his mouth. He was beside himself with joy at his wife's distress and even offered some cherries to her. In disgust, she refused them, not daring to come near.

Finally, when he could take no more of her pleas, he bit a cherry in half without looking at it himself. He turned the open side of the fruit towards his wife to show her it was worm-free as he munched the other half. She saw three thin black and white striped, severed worm bodies. They were twisting and writhing in pain around the stone of the cherry where he had bitten them off.

She pointed and tried to confirm that there were worms. She shuddered and her full-body gag reflexes kicked in. He refused to believe her, thinking she was playing a trick on him and ate the other half of the cherry without looking, worms and all.

As her knees grew weak, the wife could now hardly stand. She was so distraught over her husband eating the worms that she swore she would never kiss him again, and he laughed. Begging him again to check the fruit and actually look with his own eyes, she pleaded with everything in her.

He finally picked another cherry, bit it in half, and saw the twisting worms. He held the cherry out from him at arm's length and stared in horror. His tanned complexion went from brown to green and white as paper in less than a second.

The wife was now on the verge of a breakdown from her almost-failed attempts. She had tried and failed to save her husband from a fate almost worse than death. Seeing her husband's face turn white as he began to stagger backwards, she began to wail. He still held the cherry at arm's length.

Her wail sounded like something between howling laughter and empathetic tears of agony. He never listened to her, which frustrated her to no end, and now it seemed he was getting his "just desserts." She shrieked and howled at him not to eat anymore cherries, and he shouted at her to shut up.

He shouted at her again and again in a daze. He still gazed in horror at the wormy cherry, unable to look away. He realized how many worms he must have eaten with such gusto minutes before, and he weakened to the point that it took everything in him to remain standing.

He was hardly able to maintain consciousness as the blood left his brain. He struggled to continue shouting at her to shut up. She thought he might be exaggerating, that he was being dramatic. He staggered and struggled to remain upright. His eyes slightly crossed, and he could no longer see anything but the squirming worms in his mind's eye. He tried not to pass out.

His wife had become so distressed she could no longer stand. She fell to the ground where she rolled, laughing so hard she couldn't catch her breath. She was finally able to release her horror! She begged him to stop staggering around and shouting at her. She couldn't breathe, and he was making her laugh even more. The more she writhed on the ground, the more horrified he became.

After what seemed a long time, he was finally able to pull his wits about him, if only enough to throw the rest of the wormy half-cherry to the ground and go stomping into the house. He slammed the door behind him and left his wife alone to roll on the grass. She rocked back and forth, clutching her sides until she could get control of herself and finally stop laughing. Eventually, she wiped her face, wet from laughing so hard that she had cried, and went into the house herself.

He stayed in the bedroom with the door closed the rest of the day. His wife went about her duties as usual as if he wasn't home. She was relieved that he didn't come out so she had time to regain her composure. She promised herself she wouldn't mention the incident unless he brought it up. She didn't want to embarrass him.

Finally the husband came out for dinner. He watched his wife suspiciously to make sure she *didn't try to bring up the subject all during the meal. He was sure that she had somehow something to do with the worms being in those cherries he had eaten. But as they ate in silence, she did not bring it up and was very careful to think of other things. Without even thinking, a hilarious snort came up from her innermost depths. It tickled and betrayed her, and she could not suppress it. A joyful look came to her husband's eyes as he thought she had a funny joke or experience to tell him. She tried with great valor to push the giggle down, back down to the deep depths from which it had come.*

When he asked her to share what was so funny, he was very disappointed that she didn't want to share. She told him it was nothing and glanced away, shoveling some food into her mouth so that she could not say anything more.

They enjoyed sharing funny things with each other quite a bit, so this was not like her. More than ten minutes had gone by without incident, and she accidentally slipped another giggle. He insisted sternly that she share with him what was so funny. Instead, she told him that she was sure he didn't want to know. When he began to be angry with her, she finally told him that she couldn't help thinking about the cherries.

He slammed down his fork onto his plate and stormed back into the bedroom to sulk, even attempting to slam the bedroom door. Once he was gone, the wife burst into another fit of uncontrollable giggles at the table. For the rest of the evening she continued giggling. She waited until she was sure her husband had gone to sleep before retiring for the night.

Over the next several weeks and months this continued at random. The wife would sometimes giggle a little by pure accident. Sometimes it would happen in the car or at church. After some time, the thought only came to her mind without her giggling but he could still sense she had thought of it, and it put him into a fit of rage all over again, every time.

The cherry tree came down within the next year; revenge on the worms! The husband would never again eat another cherry, and his wife had a great story to remind him that he should listen to her. It also gave her something to look back on when he frustrated her; it helped her remember that he was just a guy who sometimes made decisions that left him with worms.

~The End~

The wife in this story used laughter to try and diffuse a stressful situation outside of her control. Rather than cry, her body chose to release the overwhelming emotion through laughter. Her attempt to lighten her husband's burden may have helped the situation from not being even worse than it was. He didn't appreciate her attempts at first but years later he found the humor in the event too.

Laughter is a powerful antidote for the body and mind to relieve stress, pain, and conflict. Nothing works faster to bring the body back into balance than a good laugh. Life can be easier if we learn to join in with others when something funny happens to us. Laughing renews us; it connects us to others and inspires our hope. Laughter keeps us grounded, alert, and lightens our burdens. It's free and easy.

Good massage therapists encourage clients to cry or laugh as these emotions come up during a session. As the body is ready to release built up emotion, it is able to process things that have been stored away. Storage of emotions happens when a feeling is so overwhelming the body can't process it at the time, both what we call good and bad emotions. The body will save the overwhelm for later when it is in an environment and time that it feels safe to proceed. This is healthy and good. Your therapist can walk you through the process and support you in your appointment.

A good, hearty laugh relieves stress in the body for almost an hour afterwards. This leaves your muscles in a relaxed state. It also increases your immune system's ability to resist disease. Laughing protects your heart and burns a few calories. It diffuses anger and sometimes conflict, decreases pain, and can even help you live longer. A study in Norway called *A 15-Year Follow-Up Study of Sense of Humor and Causes of Mortality*, Psychosomatic Medicine: April 2016, has shown that people with a strong sense of humor outlive those who don't laugh as much. (There is a huge difference for those who are battling cancer to laugh a lot compared to those who do not laugh much or at all.) As far as the social benefits go, laughter attracts others to us. It enhances teamwork and promotes group bonding.

One of the greatest blessings of laughter that many people are not familiar with is the release of anger. It helps us forgive ourselves and others. Massage therapy is integral in the forgiveness process. It helps us learn how to let go of things. Laughter helps us to overcome problems. It enhances our relationships and supports our wellness. Indeed, it is much easier to laugh with other people than alone. It is important to our life balance that we laugh with others on a regular basis.

If you have an illness, it is important to engage in lighthearted laughter with loved ones. If you are not in the practice of laughing in your daily life, you may not know where to start. Baby steps are always good. (I love baby steps!)

Smiling is easy, and often you will see others smile right back at you, which can make you feel good twice. My great uncle taught me to count my blessings instead of sheep if I had a tough time falling asleep. Do this activity any time of the day, and it will improve your mood. It changes your thought pattern toward positivity. Soon, you'll start looking for other things that make you feel good too!

People love to share funny stories like the one I shared at the beginning of this section. My grandmother always said, "If you hear people laughing about something, head on over and ask what's so funny." Most of the time, people are more than happy to repeat the story and everyone gets to laugh again.

Some people have a natural talent for laughing with ease. If you pay attention, you will discover who these people are. Spend time with them if you aren't one of those people yourself. You will find more opportunities to find humor in life yourself. Sometimes, I will ask my family about the funny things that happened to them that day. If you do the same, you will hear some great stories that way, and you all get to laugh together. It beings up funny things to share with your friends too, and they will tell you their funny stories as well.

There are funny television shows and movies that you can find. Ask people you know what their favorite comedy shows are, and you can find lots of videos online too. Developing your sense of humor can be done by reading a good joke book and sharing jokes and stories. You can read the comics in the paper, go to a comedy club, or even host a game night with friends and share funny stories. Pets are another source of goofy things to laugh about. (Look at how many funny cat videos there are.)

I've got a great story about a white long-haired cat that roamed the neighborhood. My family called it a potato cat due to its extreme plumpness and white fur. Because it was so overweight and didn't want to jump over, the cat tried to pull itself under a chain link fence gate. When it went under, it had to pull itself through by using its claws dug into the long grass on the other side. It made several mighty attempts to pull itself under our fence.

To hear the story in person will have you crying tears from laughing so hard. You'll be holding your sides for days after you hear it. I get into it and tell you everything that was happening to the cat during this process that you wouldn't expect. You feel like you were there. I'm sure that you have some great stories like this too. Make sure you have the right people around you who appreciate your sense of humor. If they don't have a sense of humor like yours you might forget you're funny because no one is laughing. Try out different types of humor to find what gets the best results.

Some of our greatest funny stories come from our most embarrassing moments. There's always a way to turn a bad situation into a funny story. Sometimes it is difficult, but you can do it. Keeping funny things around that make us laugh helps remind us to not take life too seriously.

When I was a teenager I wrote a message on my rear view mirror to smile so that I saw it every time I looked behind me. Screensavers that are funny or hanging photos up that make us laugh are great too. I'm sure the lady with the cherry-eating husband remembers that story often. It probably relieves a lot of stress for her.

Find your inner child. Children are experts at laughing and playing. They find joy in the smallest things. There are tons of YouTube videos to prove this. They think the tiniest things are hilarious. One of my ring tones on my phone is set to a baby laughing. It makes me smile every time I hear it and it has caused some humorous situations too.

Try to set aside ten to fifteen minutes every day to do something you truly enjoy that makes you laugh. Learn to avoid negative people and things. Don't seek out things that make you feel uncomfortable in a bad way, scared or frightened, depressed, or angry.

Sometimes being uncomfortable is good. It can stretch us to reach outside our comfort zone. It can help us to grow as a person. People who take life and themselves too seriously will drag you down. That will affect how you treat yourself and react to others.

Don't make the mistake of thinking someone is angry because of the way their face looks when relaxed. Learn to interpret facial expressions. Some of the most fun-loving people have what I like to call strong concentration faces. Some people who have a permanent Grinch grin at rest are actually some of the more serious people I have known. Both are often disrespected and misread by people. Take the time to get to know how people are on the inside and don't judge their funny/happy factor by their relaxed, resting face.

Remember: there is a fine line between appropriate and inappropriateness humor, and we need to know where it is. Crossing the line can hurt people's feelings and offend them. But if you work at trying to laugh every day, even if you pretend at first, it will become easier and easier. You will find you that feel better and better.

Charlie Chaplin felt like a day without laughter was a day wasted. George R.R. Martin believes that laughter is the poison to fear. Robin Williams dedicated his life to humor and blessed many people's lives. I don't know of anyone who has died from laughter, but there are a lot of people who are dying because they are *not* laughing. We should do our part to try to help spread a little laughter around and save some lives.

Life is better with laughter, and we are more resilient because of it. Resilience helps us to see failures as part of the natural progress as we work for success. Those who are not resilient see failure as a negative outcome. Resilient people are happier and more successful in life. Learn to acknowledge mistakes without becoming angry or frustrated. Being able to laugh at mistakes that we or others make is a part of being human.

Master the art of shrugging off unimportant things, and most things are not that important. Learn what is funny and what is not. Laughing at the expense of others is not funny. Be very careful about your humor and make sure to laugh *with* but not *at* people. No one likes to be picked on or made fun of, and it doesn't make you look very good, either. When it's inclusive, laughter is good, healthy, and fun.

SECTION 12
FINANCES

Page 228

I'M SURE YOU'RE WONDERING what finances have to do with healing yourself - a lot, my friend, a lot. Finances are a source of great stress for many people, and stress is the biggest reason that we need massage therapists, counselors, and doctors. Seven out of ten people are very stressed about money. Only *one* in ten is not stressed at all about their finances. No matter how much money we make, we are in a sad state of affairs if this is where we are. The number of people *greatly* stressed about money and finances is only growing. Money stress – usually not having enough - is linked to health problems, anxiety, depression, and sleeping issues.

There are many different kinds of coping mechanisms in life, and some are better than others. Some with negative side effects are: drinking alcohol, smoking, doing drugs, cutting themselves, eating disorders, and so on. (I'm sure you can think of more!) These behaviors may bring a short-lived, temporary sort of relief or numbness, but in the end, they only end up adding to or creating more stress than they started out with. This stress not only affects the person but those around them as well.

There are different consequences that go with each coping mechanism, including physical consequences to our health. We *can* learn to replace our debilitating coping mechanisms with some of the previous sections of this chapter. A good massage therapist can help you learn better habits than those with negative consequences.

When we take part in negative coping mechanisms, we have less money to spend on the basic necessities of life: wholesome food, housing, transportation, and self-care. Self-care needs to be a *daily* activity. After all, you don't wait to take your car in until everything is going wrong with it. No, you do your maintenance checks and replace things when you hit a certain mileage. You check the oil level and car fluids often so you don't run out.

Your body is *just* as important to take care of as your car, and requires a similar frequency of care. When you put things off instead of dealing with them, you are put under much greater stress. It also ends up being much more expensive in the long run and requires a lot more work to find balance again. When you are stressed, you don't sleep well. Not sleeping well affects your immune system, and you get a big sleep deficit that can't be caught up by taking naps. Sleep deficits affect our ability to think, make us moody, and so on; look how many car accidents are linked to drowsiness.

Whether from credit cards or other loans, debt creates stress. You may even feel a sense of hopelessness as the debt piles up higher and compounding interest adds to the mix. When you add debt to poor coping choices along with self-neglect it becomes too much to handle. Part of the downward spiral, this often leads to an increase in harmful behaviors. When working toward financial freedom, there are several important things to understand.

There are good classes and great shows on learning to take care of your money in a healthy way. There are too many to list in this book but check around in your local area, do a little research, and you will easily find finance experts. They will teach you how to work toward getting more of what you want out of life *without* going further into debt. First, learn how to take good care of the money that comes to you. Treat it as though it wasn't yours but lent to you to use and comes with certain rules and obligations. Understand the rules of the debt cycle and how to break out of it. Then, move toward financial freedom by following the rules and steps. This entire process can be tricky to navigate without adding to your stress, but with professional help you can get there.

If you work with someone else on your finances, get yourselves on the same page. Discuss your most basic needs, not your wants. Start with your bare necessities. Know how much money you make and how much you need to spend for these items. If you tithe, this is usually taken out first, and given to God - ten percent of your increase.

It can *feel* like you need more money in your budget, but you might be surprised how little you actually need to get by. If you are honest with yourself, you probably make enough to do that. You may not be living in the lap of luxury, but the essentials will be covered.

Most people find that if their physical and emotional needs are met, their need to "keep up with the Joneses" disappears - (no offense intended to the Jones family). Compared to many third world countries, the poor among us in the developed world are wealthy beyond measure. Create a budget to figure out where your money is going; where does it come from, and what you are doing with it? This can be a very eye-opening-experience to go through.

Learning to live on less can be a very liberating experience. Having less *stuff* to keep track of frees up a person's mental and emotional well-being too. A lot of people put emotional baggage into physical things. This can result in collecting and even hoarding, creating a protective barrier around them. When we get rid of the emotional barrier, we free up our money to do more important things. Opportunities to help those in need can be met. We can save up for retirement and provide ourselves self-care. Every one of us is in need of self-care to some degree or another. Part of learning to live on less and *with* less allows you to create a new, low-stress lifestyle.

Begin saving up a one-month emergency fund. At the same time, work towards getting insurance and emergency supplies. Even if you can only afford to save a penny a day until you are able to dedicate more to this goal, start the habit *today*.

There are various strategies that work very well for saving money. Paying for things in cash and then setting aside the change daily from your purchases is one easy idea. Plus, paying for things in cash makes us aware of how much money we are actually spending and how much we have left. Consider getting an extra part-time job. There are lots of great ideas to help you find a way to reach your goals.

Many of us live in areas prone to hurricanes, fires, floods, or drought. We all need to plan in advance for all our area's potential predicaments. Keep a supply of water on hand at all times, not just during an emergency. If you live where conditions allow, keep extra water in your car.

Toxic chemicals sometimes poison wells so people that get snowed in can't drink their well water. There are plenty of other situations where people cannot leave their homes. People who wait to the last minute to prepare will rush to the grocery store and find the shelves stripped bare already. You never know what is going to happen. Keep a supply of water on hand at all times. But be sure to have a way to sanitize your water, and rotate it out with fresh water periodically. You may even want to invest in a good water filtration system.

Food is another emergency supply you want to keep on hand. What if you can't leave your home for a week or a month? (I've been in situations like this!) What if fires or unemployment get so bad you have to live off of what is in your cupboards for three to six months? Do you have a garden growing in your yard to prepare against problems with the food delivery or money shortages?

Grocery stores only hold a day or two's worth of food. You can't rely on them as your back up food supply - and don't expect your neighbors will have anything extra, either. Do you have something to cook with if your gas or power goes out? At a previous house in which we lived, our power went out once or twice a week for three weeks straight! People kept crashing into telephone poles or the power station. It was *very* inconvenient. We never knew how long the power would out while they made repairs. We didn't dare open our fridge for fear that everything would spoil!

Several times the power was out four to six hours. It was in the middle of summer. If we hadn't had things on hand and our barbecue grill, we would have spent a lot more money out to eat and to cool off. Some of our neighbors were not so lucky. We tried to help each other as best we could and let each other know what was going on, but it was a rough month.

After saving up an emergency fund and preparing, and saving water and food, cut unnecessary debt: credit cards, consumer debt, and automobile debt. There are great ways to do this, so search around online or at your public library. Depending on your situation you may have to try different things, but it is the most amazing feeling when you get everything paid off and keep it off. That heavy burden lifts right off of you. Your quality of life also improves, even if nothing else changes.

The next step is saving and investing for the future. You already saved up a one-month emergency fund; expand that to a three-to-six month emergency fund. Keep paying down your debts, including house and college loans. Save for retirement and other special life events, including humanitarian or church missions, college, or weddings.

Last but not least: continue to give and bless others who receive. Teach your children good financial habits. Lift up those who are struggling. Help and teach them these skills. Teach them that they can support and sustain themselves to the best of their ability. These steps work whether you ask for God to help with your goal or not, but I have found great success with his love and support.

I've been working on this financial system with my husband for student loans and a car loan. Once we began working together as a united front, things got taken care of so fast. We have enjoyed the process and learned a lot about ourselves and each other. One of the greatest rewards has been the decreased stress. We're so blessed to be part of improving the lives of others in our community in various ways.

I'm sure you have some great ideas. Decide today to start reducing your stress and healing your finances. You will become a blessing to people around you. Together, we can all make a difference. We can heal our finances and ourselves through consistent and repeated baby steps.

Member, Heal Thyself!

~~~

R. Shelton, NLMT, BCTMB

R. Shelton is a licensed and board-certified bodyworker, and an expert in the wellness industry. She specializes in clinically styled bodywork of many varieties. She is dedicated to results and being an example of wellness for her clients. She loves learning new things, cooking tasty recipes and eating them, dance, music, time with loved ones, and serving in her community.

Post Your Book Review

Did you enjoy the material or learn something new? How did reading "Member Heal Thyself" impact you? Share your thoughts by leaving a heartfelt review where you bought the book.

Want to write the best review people will find helpful and love to read? The best ones are detailed and specific. How did it make you feel? What changed in your life?

Get a little personal and touch on points that other readers will find helpful too. What did you relate to? Aim for 100-150 words and break up paragraphs into 2-3 sentences for easier reading.

(If you find any typos or mistakes, don't put those in your review, instead, feel free to contact me or the publisher directly about those so we can correct them. It's impossible to catch everything even with a team of professionals looking at it but with your help we can make it perfect!)

I look forward to reading your review!

– R. Shelton

Book Recommended For:

Corporate Wellness Plans
School or University Use for Departments Of:
- Behavioral Science and Human Services
- Exercise Science
- Fitness
- Health Science
- Psychology
- Wellness Education

Class Resource Acquisitions
Book Clubs
Church Groups
Retail Stores
Health and Wellness Centers
And More

Member Heal Thyself

A much-needed book of life instructions for healing ourselves naturally. A resource that guides us to use the full potential of our physical bodies.

https://memberhealthyself.com/book

Contact Us at:
info@memberhealthyself.com
For information regarding large purchase orders